# GLORIA'S GLORIOUS MUFFINS

## GLORIA AMBROSIA

AVERY PUBLISHING GROUP INC.

Garden City Park, New York

Cover Design: Ann Vestal and Martin Hochberg
Cover Photos: John and Diane Harper
In-house Editor: Linda Comac
Typesetter: Cochran Designs, Plainedge, NY
Printer: Paragon Press, Honesdale, PA

**Library of Congress Cataloging-in-Publication Data**

Ambrosia, Gloria.
  Gloria's glorious muffins / by Gloria Ambrosia.
    p.    cm.
  Includes index.
  ISBN 0-89529-528-8 (pbk.) : $9.95
  1. Muffins.    I. Title.
  TX770.M83A45   1993                          92-41662
  641.8'15–dc20                                    CIP

Printed in the United States of America

10  9  8  7  6  5  4  3  2  1

# GLORIA'S GLORIOUS MUFFINS

Dear Bree,
    When I saw this book
I remembered the fun we had
baking "mushrooms."
    I thought you'd enjoy this!
            Love & Kisses —
                Mrs. G——

# CONTENTS

This book is dedicated to the memory of my dad, John.

Thanks for your selfless parenting, for many wonderful exchanges of truths, and especially for our chat at the kitchen table a few months before you left. You would have gotten such a kick out of all of this!

# ACKNOWLEDGMENTS

I would like to thank a number of people without whom I would not have undertaken or completed what has been a wonderful process. These are my friends and relations who share the joy of eating. First and foremost, my friend Susan for encouraging me to put pen to paper (or fingers to keyboard!) and write about my love affair with muffins. Special thanks to my mom, dad, sisters, brothers-in-law, nieces and nephews for being so supportive when I wrote my first collection of muffin recipes and for hanging in there throughout the process. Thanks to Charlotte for giving me the courage to contact publishers; to Rick for reading and critiquing the manuscript; to Nancy and Will for technical and moral support; and Barbara and Calmon and Julia and Donna and Cashin and Patty and Judy and Janice and Patti and Ken and Linda and Kenny and Randy and Steven and Douglas and George and Trish and Carey and Shanta and Jim for listening to my endless rantings about muffins and for consuming so many (!). Thanks to Boyce at Friends of the Earth for her priceless advice on natural food products; to Apple Computer for creating the Mac; and to Rudy Shur, Linda Comac, and the folks at Avery Publishing Group (what a nice bunch of people!). After all is said and done, I am convinced that there is little in life more enriching than breaking bread with friends.

# PREFACE

*Food to a large extent is what holds a society together, and eating is closely linked to deep spiritual experiences.*

Peter Farb and George Armelagos,
*Consuming Passion: The Anthropology of Eating*

When I told my family and friends I planned to write a muffin cookbook, the first question they asked was, "What are you going to do with all the test muffins?" As you can imagine, there was no shortage of people willing to sample and critique my lastest creations.

That was fine with me because, while there are many reasons I love to cook, I most enjoy seeing smiling faces and hearing the "Mmm's" of the people who eat delicious food prepared with a loving heart. Muffins have a way of calling forth the loudest "Mmm's" of all. Muffins make us happy, and when we are happy, life is a little easier.

Delighting people with muffins has become a bit of a religion with me. I imagine that my mission is to lighten people's hearts—and even turn scowls to smiles and grumbles to grins—with muffins. One of my idols is a Buddhist holy woman whose delicious cooking made a group of monks so happy that they were able to break through a stalemate in their meditation and attain the fullest fruits of their spiritual quest.

Matika-mata lived on the edge of a forest where thirty monks practiced meditation and strove toward enlightenment. Like many devout Buddhists, she would get up before dawn each day in order to prepare food for the monks' daily alms round.

One day, Matika-mata visited the monastery to receive instruction in meditation. She did as the monks had instructed and within a short period of time realized full enlightenment. It is said that her concentration was so deep that she also attained great mental powers, including the ability to read minds.

Having attained such high wisdom, she realized that none of the monks at the monastery had developed their meditation practice to the same extent. Puzzled, she used her powers of mind to probe into the mind of each monk to ascertain the reason. To her amazement, she discovered that the monks were unhappy because they were not getting the foods they liked to eat! This unhappiness dominated their states of mind and made it difficult for them to practice meditation with delight, a necessary ingredient for one who wishes to realize liberation.

Matika-mata used her powers of mind to discover each monk's favorite food. She would arise well before dawn and prepare exactly what each monk liked to eat—thirty different dishes! The monks were very happy (although they were not allowed to show it), and their happy states of mind lasted throughout the day. Before long, each monk attained the full fruits of meditation practice! Matika-mata's reputation grew, and monks came from far and wide to practice in the forest near where she lived.

Before people would come from far and wide to sample my muffins, I had to overcome one problem. I searched traditional cookbooks for interesting muffin recipes but kept finding the same, stale old ideas made the same, stale old ways. Not much had been done to make muffins interesting. And more often than not, natural-food cookbooks offer recipes for muffins that, while they may be nutritious, don't taste particularly appetizing. Plus, they are made from unfamiliar products or ingredients that are expensive or difficult to find. I decided to challenge muffins to the limits of their potential by creating interesting, nutritious, and delicious muffins made from reasonably priced and easy-to-find ingredients.

That's how this cookbook came about. I gathered together my favorite recipes, making no distinction between cakes, breads, casseroles, soups, or desserts. I even considered my favorite candy and ice cream. Then I created a muffin to capture the flavors in each. I discovered that muffins can be made out of anything. And I mean anything! And it can be done without compromising nutrition or cost. This cookbook proves it.

This cookbook *disproves* the common conception that muffins are just for breakfast. I ask you, "Why stop there?" With the right combination of ingredients and inventive serving ideas, muffins make a great dessert or after-school snack. You can take muffins along on camping trips and picnics, too. Leave out the sweetener and add veggies, herbs, or cheese and you've got great savory muffins to accompany soups, salads, or a full-course meal. And what could be more versatile for holiday meals and parties than muffins?

# PREFACE

With these ideas in mind, I developed scrumptious muffins in four categories: breakfast, savory, dessert, and holiday. Each chapter in this book presents twenty (or so) muffins and includes a variety of great serving ideas. There is a muffin for every occassion—or for no occasion at all!

Like Matika-mata, you will find, I am sure, many recipes to delight and uplift the hearts of your loved ones. But be careful. You also may find that friends and relations come from far and wide to be near you and to enjoy the fruits of your labor. While I can't guarantee that my muffins will lead to enlightenment, they will most certainly make everyone who eats them very happy.

# INTRODUCTION

*There is no love sincerer than the love of food.*
George Bernard Shaw

Muffins are on the rise, if you will pardon my pun. I mean, folks are turning in their direction. Sure, muffins have long been a favorite treat, but never more so than in recent years. With all the talk about saturated fats, high blood cholesterol, and the need for more fiber and less sugar in our diets, muffins make sense. You can use oils that are low in saturated fats, whole grains that are high in fiber, and natural unrefined sweeteners. And muffins are quick and easy to make.

I turned to muffins for all these reasons and more. You see, I have quite a history with baked goods—especially breads and sweet cakes like coffeecake and donuts. You might say we have a personal relationship. When I was a kid, I used to eat six or eight slices of raisin toast for breakfast. Mmm, mmm. My mom couldn't understand where I was putting it! Then for lunch, I'd take a couple of peanut butter sandwiches with a cream-filled cupcake or two for dessert—every day. And on Sunday mornings, my dad and I devoured a pecan coffeecake (Mmm, mmm, again!)—often forgetting to leave some for the rest of the family. When I learned in history class that the Romans conquered the world by feeding their soldiers grains and breads three times a day, I could really relate to what the soldiers had experienced. I figured that the soldiers must have been very happy people. You know what I mean? They must have *felt* as though they could conquer the world.

Over the years, I have tempered my youthful passions for gooey sweet breads and cakes made with refined ingredients. For one thing, I notice that I feel better when I have more whole-grain fiber in my diet. The bulk does my system good. I also notice that sugar highs hurt more than delight me. The overall sluggishness I experience on the heels of consuming a glazed donut is too high a price for the few moments of pleasure while eating it. Research on cholesterol consumption and its correlation with heart disease has made me take a closer look at my tendency to put gobs of butter on bread or an inch of icing on a cake made with five eggs and a cup and a half of butter.

But my sweet tooth is still with me. All my teeth are sweet! So in recent years, I've searched for baked goods that satisfy my pining for sweets without compromising my desire for good nutrition. Is it any wonder I've turned to the natural sweetness of muffins? Sometimes it's the most ordinary things in life that bring about the most extraordinary delights, isn't it?

# HELPFUL HINTS

*In the beginner's mind there are many possibilities.*
Zen Master, Suzuki Roshi

During my years of muffin-making, I have experimented with different equipment, ingredients, and procedures. Muffins are easy to make, it's true. But experience separates the mediocre muffin-makers from the fabulous ones. I've prepared this section to help you benefit from my experience and become a fabulous muffin-maker yourself. Trust me. I've worked out the kinks and can help you make better muffins.

# EQUIPMENT

*There has always been a food processor in the kitchen.*
*But once upon a time she was usually called*
*the missus, or Mom.*

Sue Berkman, *Esquire*

## Food Processor

I've always been slow to embrace new fashions (maybe even a little hard-headed), but when I come around, I'm like a religious convert. When I was a freshman in college, for example, and student government eliminated the dress code, I swore I'd never wear jeans to class. Three months later, mine were the most torn, patched, and jewel-studded jeans on campus.

I took to food processors in the same way. "Not me," I said, "I want to *feel* the food *I'm* chopping. It's strictly low tech for me." Years later, I find I can't live without my food processor. It's such a nifty little gadget. It blends, chops, grates, and pulverizes just about anything I feed it. If I feel weary or out of sorts, it smiles empathetically and says, "Let me do it for you, Sweety." I smile back gratefully and turn over the goods.

You will notice that most of my muffins are chock full of *goodies* (yummy little additions that make each muffin unique). I use my food processor to prepare most of these. If you don't have a food processor, you may want to consider investing in one. With it, muffin-making will be all the more enjoyable.

## Utensils

You need a few standard utensils—measuring cups, measuring spoons, and mixing bowls in assorted sizes. For muffins with veggies and fruit, you need a chopping surface and a sharp knife or two. A large wooden spoon is ideal for combining the wet and dry ingredients and acts as an accurate measure for spooning the batter into the muffin tins.

If you do not have a food processor, use your favorite chopping and grating utensils to prepare veggies, fruits, and nuts. Utensils such as a potato ricer (for mashing) and a hand-operated grinder (for chopping and grinding nuts and/or spices) also will come in handy. You need a wire whisk to beat the egg and mix the other wet ingredients, and a hand-held grater to grate veggies. And you need a sifter.

Despite what people say, whole-grain muffins can be relatively light and airy. One of the secrets is to sift the flour once or twice before combining it with the wet ingredients. Sifting also eliminates the clumps that are often found in baking powder, baking soda, and whole-grain flours.

You can discover the value of sifting by conducting this simple experiment. Take a cup of whole-wheat or whole-wheat pastry flour and sift it two times, measuring before and after each sifting. It grows, doesn't it? A cup of flour becomes 1 1/8—even 1 1/4 cups! You see what sifting does? It fluffs the flour, kind of like whipping cream, and that fluffiness is passed on to the final product.

"But I don't like sifting," you whine.

I know. I know. But if you don't listen to me on this one, you will have to find out the hard way. And you will have to put up with the tentative accolades of your friends and relations who haven't the heart to tell you that your whole-grain masterpieces weigh a ton. It's easier just to follow my suggestion. Get yourself a sifter. Okay?

## Muffin Tins

Unless otherwise indicated, all the recipes in this book yield a dozen muffins and require 3-inch muffin tins. It makes little difference if you use tin, iron, or no-stick pans. Baking time will be about the same. If, however, you use mini or jumbo muffin tins, you need to adjust the baking time accordingly. A standard recipe for one dozen muffins makes about three dozen mini-muffins and requires approximately 10–15 minutes baking time. A standard recipe for one dozen muffins makes six jumbo muffins and requires about 20–25 minutes baking time.

If you want to get fancy and use heart-shaped, shell-shaped, or some such whimsical tins (there are even dinosaur-shaped tins now; yes, really!), you will have to adjust the baking time accordingly. Read the manufacturer's suggestions and be willing to experiment a little. Your best bet is to watch your muffins closely as baking time will vary considerably.

## Baking Cups

Here are the pros and cons on baking cups: You can avoid the use of butter, margarine, or oil and cut down on cleanup time by using foil or paper baking cups. That's the good news.

The bad news is that warm muffins tend to adhere to the baking cups. After you peel away the paper, what's left is a crumbled core about the size of a donut hole. Very disappointing. You end up giving the muffin-coated paper to the dog and wondering if it was worth the effort of baking.

There *is* a way out. You can reduce the cling factor by cooling the muffins completely before you gobble them up.

"But," you say, "who wants to wait for them to cool?"

Admittedly, it's a dilemma. I tend not to use baking cups for this reason.

If you use *foil* baking cups, please remember that you won't be able to reheat the muffins in a microwave oven (or feed the muffin-coated paper to the dog). This could be a factor if you plan to freeze your muffins (see *Freezing and Reheating* on page 32) for later use.

# INGREDIENTS

*Tell me what you eat, and I will tell you what you are.*

Brillat-Savarin

Muffins are only quick and easy to make *if* you have the ingredients on hand. Most of the ingredients store easily and for long periods of time. I have a cupboard and a special corner in my refrigerator designated just for muffin ingredients. I try to keep these areas well stocked. My muffin staples include:

- Baking powder
- Baking soda
- Bran
- Chips: naturally sweetened carob and chocolate chips
- Coconut
- Cornmeal: blue and yellow
- Dried fruits: apples, apricots, currants, mixed dried fruit, peaches, raisins
- Eggs
- Extracts: almond, rum, strawberry, vanilla
- Flours: amaranth, brown-rice, buckwheat, millet, oat, rye, soy, unbleached white, whole-wheat, whole-wheat pastry
- Granola
- Milk: cow's milk and soy milk
- Nuts: almonds, pecans, walnuts ( I like to chop nuts and dried fruits before storing them in jars. That way, they are ready to be measured and used at a moment's notice.)
- Rolled oats
- Sea salt
- Seeds: poppy seeds, sesame seeds, sunflower seeds
- Shortening: butter, canola oil, margarine, olive oil
- Sweeteners: all-fruit jellies and jams, apple and orange juice concentrates, applesauce, barley malt, brown sugar, fresh fruit, honey, maple syrup, molasses, rice syrup, Sucanat
- Wheat germ: raw and toasted

This is only intended to be a list of most commonly used ingredients. If you find you are making muffins frequently, you will need to plan ahead and purchase the desired ingredients with your regular shopping trips.

## Flours

This is going to sound crazy but when I eat whole grains, I feel like I am eating the earth itself. Don't get me wrong. It's not that whole grains taste like dirt. It's that eating them makes me feel elementally connected with the substance of life—earth, air, heat, and water. Grains, and especially the baked goods from which they are made, are the body's ambrosia. I think that is why we feel so good inside when we eat whole grains.

For most of my muffins, I've used whole-wheat, whole-wheat pastry, and unbleached white flours because these are most readily available, and I wanted to make it easy for you to enjoy the goodness of nutritious muffins. My selection of flour depends upon the flavor, texture, and density I seek. There is no magical formula, just preference.

Up to now, you may have believed that muffins made with unrefined flours are squat, dense, and unappealing. I'm here to tell you they don't have to be. Many factors (ingredients, preparation procedures, and oven temperature) combine to determine muffin lightness. Your choice of flours is only one of them. Nutritious muffins baked with rich whole-grain flours need not have the consistency of freeze-dried lead.

If you take the time to *sift*, you can use any flour you want and still bake a relatively light muffin. You will also need to pay attention to rising agents, egg preparation, oven temperature, and amount of stirring. All of these are explained in the following pages.

If you are skittish or just plain stubborn and think that you can only produce a well-shaped muffin using unbleached white flour, suit yourself. You can substitute up to 1/2 cup unbleached white flour for the required flours in any given recipe.

But if you are willing to stretch your muffin-making efforts by trying those muffins that use a greater variety of whole-grain flours, I know you will be pleasantly surprised. Here are the flours I use and a little about each one.
**Amaranth Flour.** Amaranth is an ancient crop that is classified as a grain. It has a nutty flavor that resembles corn and is especially delicious when lightly toasted. Rich in protein (more rich even than wheat or rice) and

essential vitamins and minerals, amaranth flour contains about three grams of fat in each two-ounce serving.

Amaranth is being widely applauded as a miracle grain that will become increasingly popular in our Western diet in the years to come. Researchers have yet to work out some of the cultivation kinks. They report that the seeds are small and difficult to sow, and that parasites are difficult to control. Some sources suggest that it may be some time before we see large-scale cultivation of amaranth.

At least for the time being, it does not seem likely that amaranth flour will be sufficiently popularized to ensure low cost and ready availabilty. But it tastes so good and is so nutritious that I include it in a few of my muffins (see my Soysage Cheese, Waldorf, and Wheat Berry Surprise muffins).

Look for amaranth flour in your local health-food store. If you can't find it or don't have it readily on hand, substitute yellow cornmeal or whole-wheat flour in the muffin recipes that call for amaranth flour.

**Barley Flour.** When I learned that barley consumption has been linked with low levels of cholesterol in both humans and animals, my ears perked up. The trouble is, in order to enjoy the cholesterol-reducing properties from the grain, we need to eat it in its whole-grain form, and most of the commercially available barley and barley flour has been processed to remove the outer hull. "Pearling," as the process is called, destroys almost all the fiber and about half the barley nutrients.

Flour made from unhulled barley is available at many health-food stores. Just ask how the barley flour they sell has been prepared. If they don't have the more nutritious variety, ask if they may be willing to get it for you.

I use barley flour in muffins for its sweet taste and for the cake-like texture it provides (see my Barley Mushroom, Maple Pecan, Marvellous Marmalade, and Wheat Berry Surprise muffins). Barley flour is low in fat, containing only one gram in each two-ounce serving.

**Brown-Rice Flour.** Like barley flour, brown-rice flour is sweet to the taste, making it an ideal ingredient in breakfast and dessert muffins. People who are searching for a wheat-free diet usually turn to brown-rice flour as the principal ingredient in baked goods. It is also good for those on a low-fat diet as it has only one gram of fat in each two-ounce serving.

Brown-rice flour is made from hulled whole-grain rice, i.e., rice that has not been processed to remove the outer hull. I use brown-rice flour in combination with other flours (see my *Almond Cookie, Chai, Glazed Ginger Carrot, My Mincemeat, Old-Fashioned Ginger Currant, Peanut-Butter Rice Cake, Pumpkin Pumpkin-Seed, Spring Roll, Wheat Berry Surprise,* and *Wild Rice Stuffin'* muffins).

**Buckwheat Flour.** I have found that there are two kinds of people in the world—those who like buckwheat and those who don't. I'm one of the former. I like the way its strong, nutty flavor dominates a muffin and gives it that special taste. It is particularly delicious when combined with maple syrup. I use buckwheat flour in my *Boston Brown, Buckwheat (not Farina!),* and *Nickerpumpel* muffins.

Buckwheat flour comes in two varieties: light and dark. Light buckwheat flour is usually made from the whole seed minus the hard outer shell, while the darker variety contains both the seed and most of its hull. Dark buckwheat flour is the more nutritious of the two. In fact, it contains more protein per measure than any other kind of "grain" (buckwheat is not wheat at all; in fact, it is not even a grain; it is the seed of an herb!), and is generally the kind of buckwheat flour you find in health-food stores. If the flour has dark flecks that look something like the vanilla bean flecks in better ice creams, you know you have the dark buckwheat flour. Buy it. It's great. Buckwheat flour is very low in fat. It contains about one gram of fat in each two-ounce serving.

**Cornmeal.** Cornmeal is coarsely ground whole-kernel corn. The most common varieties are made from yellow, white, or multicolored (usually blue) corn. Yellow cornmeal is slightly more nutritious than its sister variety, white cornmeal. I use it in my *Boston Brown, Chili Beanie, Cornmeal Mush and Seeds, Mexicali Corn, Nickerpumpel,* and *Proof-of-the-Pudding* muffins. I use blue or yellow cornmeal in my *Blue Morning Muffins.*

In the process of grinding the corn into flour, many manufacturers remove the hull and the germ from the grain. These are the most nutritious parts of the corn, so shop for stone-ground or water-ground cornmeal. These processes ensure that the germ is retained, and also diminish the crumble factor quite common in muffins made from degermed cornmeal. Cornmeal contains about two grams of fat in each two-ounce serving.

**Millet Flour.** I first ate millet many years ago in a millet and lentil loaf that my friend Annie used to make. (I created my *Spinach-Lentil Muffins* to mimic the flavors in this wonderful loaf.) I liked millet so much that I began enjoying it on its own as an occasional substitute for rice. (What I like most is the way my body feels after eating it.) Millet is noticeably fluffier and more digestible than other grains, and its light texture makes it a welcome addition to muffins.

Finely ground millet, or millet flour, is particularly high in minerals and has a more nearly complete protein than other grains. It contains two grams of fat in each two-ounce serving. In addition to my *Spinach-Lentil Muffins*, I use millet flour in my *Artichoke Hearts*, *Fakin' Bacon*, *Polka Dottie*, and *Wheat Berry Surprise* muffins.

**Rolled Oats and Oat Flour.** Oats are prepared for popular consumption by flattening the whole grain, or groat, into a disk. Rolling, as the process is called, makes the oats easier to cook but does not rob the grain of any of its nutritional value. I use rolled oats in my *Eat-Your-Oatmeal* and *Wheat Berry Surprise* muffins.

The popular breakfast cereal granola is made from rolled oats. Granola was one of the first health-food-type cereals to take the leap from specialty food stores into the commercial market. But there is one word of caution about granola. While oats themselves are very low in fat, when the oats are mixed with oils, nuts, seeds, soy flour, and (sometimes) coconut to make granola, the end product can be a relatively high-fat cereal. Check the fat content in the brand of granola you buy. There are brands in which manufacturers have cut back on high-fat ingredients. If you make your own granola, use low-fat oils and limit the use of nuts and coconut. Depending on what granola you use, my *Gloria's Granola* and *Seven-Factors-of-Enlightenment* muffins may not be particularly low in fat.

Oat groats can also be ground to a flour that brings the wonderful flavor of oats, but not the lumpy appearance, to muffins. And oat flour contains only one gram of fat in each two-ounce serving. I use oat flour in my *Blueberry Blintze* and *Gloria's Granola* muffins. Muffins made with oat flour tend to stay fresh a little longer because the flour contains a natural antioxidant.

**Rye Flour.** Like other types of flour, rye is milled in several ways. Light and medium rye flours have had the bran and/or germ removed and, therefore, much of the nutritional value. Dark rye flour is made from whole rye berries and has the nutrition of whole-grain rye intact. Rye flour contains about one gram of fat in each two-ounce serving.

Even though rye flour enjoys only limited use in this country, it is popular enough to be sold commercially. You can find it in major grocery stores next to the whole-wheat flours and cornmeals. Most commercial brands of rye flour, however, are primarily wheat—so check the labels to be sure that the product contains only rye flour or (at least) that the rye is listed first among the ingredients.

I use rye flakes (whole rye grain that has been rolled to flatten it) in my *Jewish Rye Muffins*. I use rye flour in them, too, and in my *Boston Brown*, *Nickerpumpel*, *Seedy*, and *Wheat Berry Surprise* muffins. If you like rye flour and want to use it more frequently, substitute as much as 1/3 cup of it in any of my muffin recipes.

*Soy Flour.* I have to admit that I find soy flour tastes a tad bitter and that it tends to weigh heavily in muffin batter. In addition, it tends to dry a muffin and increase the crumble factor. Soy flour can also be quite high in fat. The fat content ranges anywhere from one gram in each two-ounce serving of *defatted* soy flour, to about six or seven grams in *low-fat*, and as much as twelve to fourteen grams in each two-ounce serving of *full-fat* soy flour. But because it boosts the nutritional power (especially protein content) of muffins dramatically, I've used it in several of my muffins (see *Charity Nut*, *Chutney*, *Cucci Cucci Couscous*, *Down-to-Earth Date and Nut*, *Falafel*, *Ladda's Lemon Ginger*, *Nickerpumpel*, *Sea-Veggie*, and *Seedy muffins*).

If you want the added nutrition and don't mind a slightly heavier muffin, try substituting a tablespoon or two of soy flour for the flour in any muffin recipe in this book. In those recipes where I have already used a heavy flour such as amaranth, buckwheat, or millet, you would be wise to substitute the soy flour for some of the heavy flour rather than for the unbleached white, whole-wheat pastry, or whole-wheat flours.

Some soy flours on the market have been heat treated or slightly toasted to improve the flavor and aid digestibility. When buying soy flour, ask for these.

**Wheat Flour.** Wheat is the number one grain crop in this country. The white bread you and I "enjoyed" as kids (and many people still "enjoy" today) was made from white *wheat* flour–ground wheat berries that had been milled to remove the bran and germ, and most of the nutrition. This was and still is done for a number of reasons–to reduce spoilage, to increase elasticity, and to refine the texture. Interestingly, the removed bran and germ (the most nutritious parts of the berries) are fed to animals while the least nutritious parts are reserved for humans. Sort of backwards, isn't it?

In addition to excessive milling, white flour is bleached. Both the milling and the bleaching diminish the nutritional value of the wheat.

What we call whole-wheat flour is made by milling the whole-wheat berry or seed to a powder. The end product is a highly nutritious and versatile flour that constitutes a major part of the fiber in our diets. Whole-wheat flour contains about two grams of fat in each two-ounce serving.

Not all whole-wheat flour on the market is *whole* wheat. Often manufacturers remove the germ and some of the bran to retard spoilage. Check the label to make sure that you are buying 100 percent whole-wheat flour.

I've used wheat flours in all of my muffins. In many muffins, I use whole-wheat pastry flour. This is whole-wheat flour made from soft wheat that has been milled a little longer to give it a finer consistency. And in some recipes, I use unbleached white flour for its light consistency. In these recipes, I often add a few tablespoons of wheat germ or bran to put the nutrition back in.

## Rising Agents (Bicarbonate of Soda and Baking Powder)

To get muffins to rise, you need a rising agent. Baking powder gives the quickest rising action, and you will find that I use it in nearly all my recipes. The exceptions are those recipes with ingredients high in acid. You see, baking powder is produced by combining acid (cream of tartar) and alkaline (bicarbonate of soda) powders. When these two meet in moist environments, they give off a lot of hot air. The hot air, carbon dioxide, is what makes the muffins rise. If the recipe uses ingredients that are already high in acid, it's best to use just bicarbonate of soda or a combination of powder and soda. And that's what I have done.

When buying rising agents, bear in mind that they do not have a long shelf life. If your muffins are consistently turning out flat and squat, it's probably because your rising agent is flat and squat. Throw it out and buy a fresh supply. If you bake infrequently, buy small packages.

If you reach for baking powder and find that you have run out—not to worry. Mix cream of tartar and bicarbonate of soda, two-to-one, and measure the mixture as you would baking powder. It's essentially the same thing.

One word of caution about baking powder . . . some commercial baking powders contain sodium aluminum sulfate or just plain aluminum. Recent studies revealed that people with Alzheimer's disease have high concentrations of aluminum in the damaged areas of their brains. No one knows for sure if aluminum in the brain is the cause or the effect of Alzheimer's, but until the issue is cleared up, I think it's best to avoid using sodium aluminum sulfate. Don't you?

## Sea Salt

You will notice that I use sea salt instead of table salt in my muffins . I began using sea salt a few years ago when I starting paying more attention to my diet. I learned that table salt is pure sodium chloride with iodine. Table salt is generally mined from inland deposits that are millions of years old. All the valuable trace minerals have long since evaporated. In addition, commercially processed salt includes a number of less-than-healthful additives designed to purify the salt and make it more free-flowing.

Sea salt, on the other hand, is salt that has been produced by natural evaporation of sea water. It is rich in trace minerals and usually contains no additives. (The whiter the sea salt, the more additives it contains.) You can buy sea salt at your health-food store. It costs more than table salt, but with the little bit we use, it is worth it.

If you prefer to use regular table salt, substitute an equal amount for the sea salt.

## Sweeteners

What more can be said about refined sugar? We all know the facts. It's nil on nutrition and sky high on calories. It offers a nice little boost, and then plummets us into physical and emotional depression. Yuk! Yet who among us hasn't acquired such a taste for it that we feel deprived or disappointed when we try to cut it out of our diets, or just cut back on its use?

One of my biggest motivations in creating muffin recipes and writing this cookbook has been to provide nutritious but sweet muffins that can take the place of the less-than-wholesome snacks, breads, and cakes that most of us have become accustomed to eating. That means using natural sweeteners that are not refined or contaminated by additives and preservatives, and that have not been overly processed.

Part of the charm and appeal of muffins is that they can be made without processed or refined sugars (without much sweetener at all, for that matter) and still convince the "kid" in us that we're getting sticky, gooey sweets. Horray for muffins!

Here's how it's done. I make my muffins with all kinds of natural sweeteners from syrupy treats like honey, molasses, barley malt, rice syrup, and maple syrup to the whole array of fruit sweeteners including whole fresh fruit, unsweetened applesauce, all-fruit jelly, fruit juice concentrate, and dried fruit. Fruit is rich in vitamins and minerals and it provides natural sweetness. I also use a newly popularized product called Sucanat. It has the texture and taste of brown sugar but without the intense processing.

Another of my sweet secrets is to incorporate citrus rind into many of my muffin recipes. It has a way of making muffins taste light and apparently sweet. My *Irish Soda Muffins*, for example, use both raisins and orange rind and contain no other sweetener. Yet they are totally satisfying.

Many people will argue that sugar is sugar is sugar, and that it makes no difference to the body if it comes from refined white table sugar or whole fresh fruit. These arguments fail to consider two important factors.

First, refined is refined is refined. Why eat refined sugars when whole sweeteners—those that have not been altered for mass production—are available? It makes good nutrition sense to make use of the *natural* sugars in fruits, grains, honey, and sugar cane. (See Table 1.1 on page 19 to see how these sweeteners compare to table sugar.)

Second, Americans have gone bananas with their sugar consumption. (Government statistics regarding our consumption of sugar state that in 1820, Americans consumed 10 pounds of sugar each year; in 1870, 20 pounds; in 1910, 87 pounds; and by the end of the 1980's, 125 pounds per year, per individual!) We are now faced with the difficult task of reversing this alarming trend. It is not likely that we are going to do that overnight.

Muffins make it possible for us to enjoy the sweet breakfast and dessert cakes that we have become accustomed to eating, but without the heavy dose of sugar. Because sweeteners from natural sources tend to be more bulky (and in some cases, more sweet), we can use less of the following sweeteners:

**All-Fruit Jam, Jelly, and Marmalade.** Not long ago, only specialty and health-food stores carried all-fruit jams, jellies and marmalades—and the price was sky high! But the buzz about too much sugar in our diets has become such a common concern that we are increasingly seeing these products manufactured by major jelly companies and sold in regular food markets. They are still more expensive than jellies made with refined sugar, but I have noticed that even during the months it took to prepare this cookbook, the prices have been slowly dropping. I also noticed that several of the chain grocery stores in my area now offer all-fruit jelly products with their own labels and at lower prices.

All-fruit jams, jellies, and marmalades are sweetened with fruit juice concentrates such as white grape and apple. They generally contain no preservatives, no artificial coloring, and no artificial flavor.

**Barley Malt Syrup.** Malted barley (sprouted, unhulled barley) can be treated with an acid solution and heated to form a concentrated, thick, and gooey sweetener. Because it is prepared in this way, I suppose one could say it isn't really natural. But the fact that barley malt syrup is made from a whole grain and contains scant amounts of nutrients not contained in other sweeteners, makes it an attractive sweetening agent for some people. Barley malt syrup is one of two grain syrups I have used in my muffins (the other is rice syrup). Because it is quite heavy, I use it sparingly; and because it is not widely enjoyed, I always recommend an alternative sweetener in those recipes where I use barley malt syrup.

I also use malted milk powder in a few of my muffins. It adds a distinctive sweet flavor that I find appealing. Malted milk powder is made by mixing barley malt syrup with milk and evaporating the moisture. It is available in regular food markets, next to, or near, chocolate milk powders and syrups.

**Dried Fruit.** Almost all fruits can be dried either naturally (under the sun) or with artifically generated heat. When added to muffins, dried fruits can reduce or eliminate the need for other sweeteners.

Another beauty of using dried fruits is that they are readily available year round. The more common fruits—apples, apricots, dates, peaches, pears, prunes—are produced by major fruit-preserving companies and are available in regular food markets (next to the raisins).

**Fruit.** I often use fresh fruit or applesauce as a sweetener. Besides being nutritious, it is a great source of dietary fiber. When a muffin recipe calls for fruit, *whole fresh fruit* is best. I indicate if canned or frozen fruit can be substituted when a particular fresh fruit is not in season.

**Fruit Juice.** I use apple or orange juices in many of my muffins. These are readily available in commercial markets. Check the labels to make sure that they do not contain added sugar. When a recipe calls for orange juice, you can maximize nutrition by using freshly squeezed.

*Fruit Juice Concentrate.* When buying fruit juice concentrates, check the ingredients to make sure they do not contain sugar. You will be pleased to discover that many of the frozen juice concentrates these days contain no added sugar.

*Honey.* Honey cannot be said to be high in nutrition. It contains only small quantities of minerals and trace elements. Chemically, it is much like table sugar. But there are other reasons to use honey instead of sugar. First, honey is twice as sweet as refined sugar so we tend to use less. Second, honey adds moisture so we can use less fat. This is especially true in baking. Third, honey's sweetness comes from sugars that are absorbed into the body more slowly than table sugar and so provide a steadier supply of energy. And, fourth, when purchased from non-commercial sources, honey is a natural and unprocessed food.

The light colored honeys—orange blossom, clover, tupelo, and alfalfa—are lightest in texture. They have the least obtrusive flavors when used in muffins. Buckwheat, the darkest honey commonly available, is the most nutritious. It can, however, overpower the flavor of muffins. You may want to consider these points when buying honey for your muffins.

*Maple Syrup.* When I was a kid, the regular grocery store sold pure maple syrup for our pancakes and waffles. At that time, it seemed that all the different brands of syrup on the shelf were pure, or nearly so. I've noticed that over the years, pure maple syrup has been slowly replaced by crazy mixed-up substitutes consisting of mostly corn syrup and very little (if any) pure maple syrup. Some products do not even use the word "maple" in the name. They are called "table syrup"!

Do yourself a *flavor.* Buy the real stuff.

*Molasses.* Molasses is the big daddy of natural sweeteners because it contains the most significant amounts of nutrients. It is actually a by-product of the sugar refining process. At each stage in the three-step process, syrup is separated from the sugar crystals and a progressively darker, thicker, and less sweet syrup—the various kinds of molasses—remains. As you might imagine, many of the nutrients that are removed from sugar cane to produce refined sugar remain in the molasses.

Most molasses sold commercially comes from the first or second stage of the refining process. Either one works well with muffins. Blackstrap molasses, the darkest syrup coming from the final stage, is not the best bet for our needs.

Molasses has a distinctive, old-time flavor that goes particularly well with spices like ginger, cinnamon, and nutmeg. There's nothing quite like it.

**Rice Syrup.** Rice syrup has a wonderful flavor. I have become so good at detecting it that I can usually tell right away if a natural confection has been sweetened with rice syrup. It is delicious! But . . . can we talk . . . It is outrageously expensive. I use it sparingly.

Rice syrup is made from fermented rice that has been boiled and evaporated until a sweet syrup remains. The process is similar to that used in making barley malt.

**Sucanat.** Sucanat is a fairly new product (new in this country, that is). It is made by evaporating the water from sugar cane juice. The result is a pure, natural sweetener with all the nutrients of the sugar cane.

Sucanat tastes and handles much like dark brown sugar. I find it particularly delicious as an ingredient in crumb topping or in recipes where I might formerly have used brown sugar. It contains no chemicals, preservatives, or artificial ingredients. For a while, I could only find Sucanat at health-food stores and it was very expensive. But I discovered that some supermarket chains carry it. You can find it on the shelf right next to the refined white sugar! It is still about three times as expensive as refined white sugar, but remember, you will use less because you will use it in conjunction with other natural sweeteners. I think it's a great product and predict we will be seeing more of it.

You may notice that I have limited the use of rice syrup and barley malt. These two natural grain sweeteners are applauded as wholesome and nutritious substitutes for honey. But because they are less than half as sweet as honey, I need to use too much to get the sweetness I desire and still produce light muffins. Besides, I find the cost prohibitive. A one-pound jar of rice syrup costs about $4.50 and a one-pound jar of barley malt costs about $3 as compared to only $1 for the same size jar of honey. At some point, my purse becomes as much a factor as palate and nutrition. I include barley malt and rice syrup in this cookbook, however, for people who cannot use other sweeteners.

Table 1.1 shows how natural sweeteners compare to table sugar, and demonstrates the relative sweetness of natural sweeteners. I recommend, however, that if you wish to make substitutes for the sweeteners I have used in my recipes, you proceed with caution and common sense. Replacing 1/2 cup warmed molasses or 1/2 cup maple syrup for 1/2 cup warmed honey will not change the texture of the batter, but will change the flavor considerably. Substituting 2 1/2 cups fruit juice for 1/2 cup honey will not change the flavor very much, but will require a significant increase in dry ingredients. Certain substititutions should not be attempted, for example, substituting dried fruit for fruit juice concentrate.

| Table 1.1 | Sweetners Equal to One Cup Refined Table Sugar |
|---|---|
| 1 cup | all-fruit jam, jelly, and marmalade |
| 1 1/4 cups | barley malt syrup |
| 1 1/2 cups | dried fruit |
| 2 1/2 cups | fruit juice |
| 3/4 cup | fruit juice concentrate |
| 1/2 cup | honey |
| 1/2 cup | maple syrup |
| 1/2 cup | molasses |
| 1 1/4 cups | rice syrup |
| 3/4 cup | Sucanat |

## Dairy and Soy Products

If you are a strict vegetarian, you will be pleased to know that most of my recipes make it easy to enjoy a dairy-free muffin. Wherever possible or appropriate, I list *both* dairy and soy products in my recipes. Soy milk and cow's milk can be used interchangeably. (See *Diary Products vs. Soy Products* on page 20 for further discussion of the soy/dairy question.)

If you decide to use soy milk, there are a few things you should know. Much of the packaged soy milk on the market is expensive and contains vanilla, cane juice, barley malt, or similar extras. These are added to reduce

# Diary Products vs. Soy Products

*It's something to sneeze about.*

Gloria Ambrosia

Personally, I think there is nothing more boring than listening to people crusade about the latest trend in health and nutrition. And no conditions are more wobbly and inconsistent than the trends themselves. But I have to tell you that two factors made me listen up and consider reducing my dairy intake by substituting with soy products wherever possible.

First, the United States Department of Agriculture (USDA) recently published a reorganization of the four basic food groups from a *food wheel* into a *pyramid*. (See Figure 1.1.) While the wheel represents the four basic food groups in a manner that suggests that each group is of equal importance in our diets, the pyramid indicates that the food groups should be prioritized with grains, fruits, and vegetables in the most favorable positions. Meat and dairy products are not highly favored, implying that we would be wise to cut down, if not significantly reduce, our consumption. As you might expect, the pyramid has caused a ruckus within the cattle and dairy industries.

But it wasn't only the USDA publication that convinced me. I had suffered for several months from an acute allergy. A friend suggested that I try reducing my intake of dairy products—"just as an experiment," she said with subtle persuasion. I did, and the condition improved immediately!

I realize this book is about muffins not who's who and what's what with hay fever and the USDA, but I was so impressed by these points that I just had to pass them on. Now you know why I list both dairy and soy products in my recipes wherever possible.

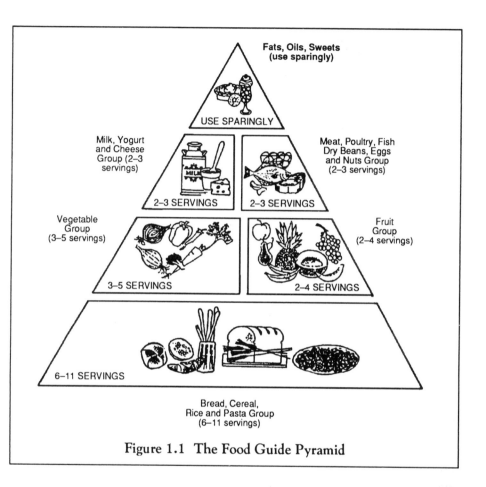

Figure 1.1  The Food Guide Pyramid

the chalky flavor and make soy milk more palatable for people who drink it as a beverage. But you do not need the more expensive varieties with all the extras. Plain old unflavored soy milk will do. It is less expensive and actually more desirable for baking as it does not add flavors that you may not want. I mix my own soy milk from packaged soy milk powder. (You can buy it at your local health-food store.) There are several brands on the market, each with mixing directions clearly stated on the package.

## Shortening

What to do about shortening? Do we use butter, margarine, or oil? And how do we know which kinds are the best to use? These are not easy questions to answer.

As Americans, we have the dubious distinction of enjoying the highest level of cardiovascular disease (particularly heart attack and stroke) in any country on the planet. Many Americans have comparatively high levels of cholesterol in their blood due largely to an excessive consumption of saturated fat and cholesterol itself. (For more on the topic, see *A Bit on Fat and Cholesterol in Our Diets* on page 24.)

There is a tremendous amount of research and literature on the subject, most of it conflicting. Even among cookbooks known to be health conscious, opinions and viewpoints range from scrupulous avoidance of saturated fats and certain unsaturated fats to wholesale sanctioning of butter and certain margarines. Many people complain of being confused—and it is no wonder!

I am of the opinion that it is better to be safe than sorry. There are saturated and unsaturated fats in so many other foods we eat and in so many hidden forms that at least we can be sure of what is in our muffins. Right?

I use canola oil in most of my breakfast, dessert, and holiday muffins, and olive oil or canola oil in my savory/dinner muffins. These oils, as seen in Table 1.2, are among the lowest in saturated fats of all commonly used cooking oils. Safflower, soybean, corn, and sunflower oils have comparably low levels, too—so use them if you prefer.

If you love the flavor of butter or margarine, can't imagine baked goods without them, and can afford the saturated fat in your diet, you can substitute butter or margarine for the oils I have suggested. One cup of oil equals one cup of melted butter or margarine. But if you want to keep your intake of saturated fat to a minimum, stick with the oils I have suggested and avoid spreading butter or margarine on the final product.

## Eggs

If you are concerned about cholesterol, take note: The muffin recipes in this cookbook call for only one egg per dozen muffins. I have tried to make my muffins without eggs but, with rare exceptions, have not been pleased with the results. Egg in muffin batter serves two purposes: It participates in the rising action, and it helps glue the muffin together. In some cases, the ingredients are such that the rising agent alone can do the job of rising,

Table 1.2   Comparison of Fats and Oils

| Kind of oil (1 tbsp.) | Saturated (grams) | Unsaturated (grams) | Polyunsaturated (grams) |
|---|---|---|---|
| canola oil | 0.9 | 7.6 | 4.5 |
| safflower oil | 1.2 | 1.6 | 10.1 |
| sunflower oil | 1.4 | 6.2 | 5.5 |
| corn oil | 1.7 | 3.3 | 8.0 |
| olive oil | 1.8 | 9.9 | 1.1 |
| margarine, liquid, bottled | 1.8 | 3.9 | 5.1 |
| margarine, soft, tub | 1.8 | 4.8 | 3.9 |
| sesame oil | 1.9 | 5.4 | 5.7 |
| soybean oil | 2.0 | 3.2 | 7.9 |
| margarine, stick | 2.1 | 5.1 | 3.6 |
| peanut oil | 2.3 | 6.2 | 4.3 |
| palm oil | 6.7 | 5.0 | 1.3 |
| butter | 7.1 | 3.3 | 0.4 |
| coconut oil | 11.8 | 0.8 | 0.2 |

Sources: United States Department of Agriculture. Science and Education Administration. *Composition of Foods: Fats and Oils–Raw • Processed • Prepared.* Agriculture Handbook 8-4, June 1979.
United States Department of Agriculture. Human Nutrition Information Service. *Composition of Foods: Legumes and Legume Products–Raw • Processed • Prepared.* Agriculture Handbook 8-16, December 1986.

and/or the muffins will hold together without egg. I have left the egg out of such recipes or given you the option to do so.

If you are on an egg-free diet you may want to use only the egg white or an egg substitute. (If you are also on a dairy-free diet, read the ingredients of egg substitutes carefully. Most contain non-fat milk powders.) You can use egg substitutes without affecting the consistency of the muffins in this cookbook. Follow manufacturers directions for use in baking.

# A Bit on Fat and Cholesterol in Our Diets

*But wait a bit, the Oysters cried,*
*Before we have our chat.*
*For some of us are out of breath,*
*And all of us are fat !*

Lewis Carroll,
*Through the Looking Glass*

**Fat.** Fat is an essential building block of life. Despite what most people think, we need fat in our diets. It provides fuel for the body, keeps us warm, and helps in the assimilation and transport of important nutrients to the cells of the body.

Like sugar, however, fat is being consumed in excess. Americans' consumption of fat has skyrocketed from less than the recommended 30 percent twenty years ago to nearly 40 percent today. Researchers say that our excessive consumption of specific types of fat is the primary cause of increased rates of heart disease, obesity, and certain cancers.

**Cholesterol.** Cholesterol is a fat-like substance found in all the cells in our bodies. It, too, is an essential component of body chemistry, making up part of each cell membrane. Because most of the cholesterol in our bodies is produced by our cells, we need little if any cholesterol in the *foods* we eat.

Cholesterol has been the subject of much concern in recent years. Studies have shown that excessive levels of cholesterol in the blood can lead to clogging of the arteries and an insufficient flow of blood to the heart.

**Choose a Diet Low in Saturated Fat and Cholesterol.** Fat in our food takes three forms: saturated, monounsaturated, and polyunsaturated. Saturated fats are usually solid when stored at room temperature and tend to increase the amount of cholesterol in the blood. Unsaturated fats (mono- and polyunsaturated) usually take the form of oils at room temperature and don't seem to have much effect on the cholesterol level. If anything, they seem to lower blood cholesterol.

Because of the strong association between the consumption of saturated fat and cholesterol and the rate of cardiovascular disease, the USDA recommends that we maintain a diet that is *low* in saturated fat and *low* in cholesterol. For people who are overweight or at high risk for cardiovascular disease, fat and cholesterol consumption is a particularly serious matter and strict guidelines should be followed. But for others, more flexibility is considered appropriate.

If you know that your cholesterol level is high and that your diet tends to be high in saturated fats, available information seems to indicate that you would be wise to lower your intake of saturated fats. But if your cholesterol levels are not high and your diet is not particularly fatty, then you have more leverage in choosing what to eat.

## Orange and Lemon Rind

Citrus rind is one of my magic ingredients. You will find that I use it quite frequently. It has a way of adding that little something extra and really enhancing the flavor of muffins.

If you make muffins often, you may want to keep citrus rind on hand at all times. I prepare citrus rind whenever it's most convenient. For example, if a recipe calls for lemon juice but not the rind, I take that opportunity to prepare the rind for muffins. Or if I eat an orange, instead of throwing away the rind, I prepare it for muffin recipes. (See page 28 for preparation directions.)

Commercial brands of orange and lemon rind can be found in the spice section of your local grocery store. I don't recommend them. If you have ever used the real thing, you know why. Prepared commercial brands just don't have the oomph.

# PROCEDURES

*Learn to labor and to wait.*

Henry Wadsworth Longfellow, "A Psalm of Life"

Your equipment is assembled. Your ingredients are on hand. Will a marriage of the two be made in heaven? It will be if you follow the proper procedures.

## Setting Oven Temperature

If you've ever made muffins that look like flying saucers or the leaning tower of Pisa, you've probably used too cool or too hot an oven. Muffins require a hotter oven than most cakes and breads. If you are having problems with flat muffins or uneven peaks (see *Figure 1.2*), test the thermostat in your oven.

Figure 1.2   **Peaks on baked muffins.** Correctly baked muffins will be straight-sided and slightly rounded on top (left). When oven heat is too low, muffins will be flat (center). If oven is too hot, muffin will have uneven peaks (right).

For the best results, the rising action must be quick and to the point, so preheating is essential. Bake all muffins at 400°F unless I have indicated otherwise. (Muffins containing large amounts of fruit tend to burn before they are thoroughly baked. These I cook more slowly.)

## Wet / Dry Preparations

Keep preparations simple. That's the beauty of muffins. With few exceptions, my muffins are quick and easy enough to make for breakfast or, even at the last minute, as a welcome addition to dinner. I keep it simple by preparing the wet and dry ingredients separately and combining them just as

I am ready to pop my muffins into the oven. You will need two bowls *or* one or two bowls and a food processor. Always pour the wet ingredients into the dry ingredients, not the other way around. Otherwise you will have to stir too much.

## Working With Your Food Processor

As stated earlier, working with a food processor can make muffin-making a snap. Follow these simple procedures:

**To grate.** Scraped knuckles and broken fingernails can be a thing of the past if you use a food processor instead of a hand-held grater to grate fruit, veggies, and cheese. I use either the grating attachments or the purée blade, depending on what I want to grate. For example, I use the purée blade to "grate" citrus rind (see *Citrus Rind Preparation* on page 28), ginger root, or garlic (see *Ginger Root and Garlic Preparation* on page 29), and the grating attachments to grate veggies and most cheeses.

Most food processors come with two grating blades—a large one that produces long, plump, and stringy results, and a smaller one for fine, feathery results. I tend to use the larger blade for cheese because it's easier on the machine (and the long strings of cheese are going to melt into the muffin anyway), and the smaller blade for veggies like carrots and squash (because the fine grating is a more appropriate size for muffins).

When you use the grating attachments to grate cheese, there are two precautions. First, some food processors just do not have the power to grate soft cheese. If you notice that your machine is whining and moaning when you try to grate soft cheese, *stop*. You may force the machine to work so hard that it burns itself out. For soft cheese, cut the cheese into half-inch chunks and "grate" using the purée blade. Simply attach the purée blade and put the chunks into the food processor. Pulse ("momentary" setting) and the cheese will break up into smaller bits. Second, when using the grating attachment for grating hard cheese, be sure that the cheese has been well chilled. Hard cheese will grate best if you use the larger grating attachment.

Always measure the ingredients *after* grating. (You can make it easy on yourself by buying pre-grated cheese for my muffins.)

**To chop.** I use the purée blade to chop nuts, seeds, fresh fruit, dried fruits, and veggies. Simply equip the machine with the purée blade, place the item to be chopped into the food processor (you will need to chop large fruit and veggies into chunks first), and turn it on. You can control the amount of chopping (from coarse to fine) by using the pulse button and pulsing in short spurts until you reach the desired results. The line between *chopped* and *gooey* is a thin one. Be careful not to overdo.

**To mash and purée.** This is the most foolproof use of the food processor. It is difficult to *over* mash or *over* purée. Use the purée blade to mash or purée such ingredients as pumpkin and sweet potatoes. Add water as needed to achieve the desired consistency.

**To blend.** When a recipe requires that I grate, chop, or purée one or more of the ingredients in the food processor, I also use the food processor to blend the wet ingredients. If, however, the recipe does not require the use of the food processor, I tend to blend the wet ingredients by hand, using a wire whisk. The purée blade is especially handy when combining thick ingredients like peanut butter or tahini with the remaining wet ingredients.

**To clean up.** Some people complain that using a food processor requires too much cleanup. I find the opposite is true. There is no reason to rinse the processor parts after each step in a recipe. Why bother? All the ingredients are going into the same muffin. Right? If you plan your chopping and grating carefully, as I have done, you should only have to rinse your machine once. Easy prep. Easy cleanup. That's the beauty of making muffins.

## Citrus Rind Preparation

Here's how to prepare citrus rind: Remove all the pulp and cut away as much of the pith (the white stuff) as possible. Break the rind into 1/2-inch pieces. Using the purée blade of your food processor, finely grate the rind.

You can grate the rind from several pieces of fruit at once, and store it in a glass jar or plastic container in the refrigerator. Stored this way, citrus rind will keep for several weeks.

## Ginger Root and Garlic Preparation

I use a fair amount of both ginger root and garlic in my muffins. To prepare ginger root, peel away the hard outer surface and slice the root into 1/2-inch pieces. Using the purée blade of your food processor, finely "grate" the ginger root. To prepare garlic, peel away the papery outer layer from the garlic cloves. Using the purée blade of your food processor, finely mince the garlic, several cloves at a time.

You can grate ginger root or garlic 1/4–1/2 cup at a time and store in glass jars or plastic containers in the refrigerator. Stored this way, it, too, will keep for several weeks.

## "Goody" Preparations

So many of my recipes have lots of added ingredients that I usually prepare the goodies separately. I measure and mix goodies, then add them to the wet or dry ingredients (whichever the recipe says to do) and mix again. This helps cut down on the amount of stirring needed after you combine the wet and dry ingredients, and it helps distribute the goodies evenly throughout each muffin.

## Mixing

It is very important to mix the wet ingredients thoroughly before combining them with the dry. Once the wet and dry ingredients are combined, stirring must be kept to a minimum if you want muffins with the proper texture. If the batter is beaten for too long, the muffin will be coarse with tunnels running through it (see Figure 1.3).

**Figure 1.3  Muffin resulting from overly beaten batter.**

If you are a bread-maker or cake-baker you may need to adjust your thinking. You are probably accustomed to long periods of beating and kneading to obtain a smooth, lump-free batter. Muffins are best when *mixed as little as possible*. With muffins, lumps are good, smooth is bad.

Having said that, I must add that there *is* a balance. It is important not to understir or you may find clumps of flour in your muffins. The batter should be thick and not runny. It should require that you *spoon* rather than *pour*. I promise you will get the hang of it. It just takes a little experience.

## Greasing the Muffin Tins

Whatever size tins you use, be sure to grease them generously with butter, margarine, or oil, or line the tins with baking cups (see *Baking Cups* on page 6.).

If you use butter or margarine, smear it liberally in each cup. You can use your fingers, a paper towel, or napkin. Spread a little over the lip of each cup as well. My recipes have been calculated to yield large dome-shaped muffins that expand over the top of each cup. Greasing the lip of the baking cups will make it easy for you to remove the muffins after they have baked.

If you grease with oil, make sure it's the same type of oil that is used in the muffin recipe. Using a paper towel or a pastry brush, smear the oil in each muffin tin and on the lip of each cup.

No-stick cooking sprays probably are desirable for people on fat- or cholesterol-restricted diets. However, I avoid using them for three reasons: While I know that the manufacturers have improved the spray cans to make them more environmentally friendly, my lungs have yet to adapt. I cough and sputter every time I spray. And when I bite into my nice, hot, fresh-baked muffin, the first thing I taste is the unappetizing flavor of no-stick spray. Yuk! Finally, when I used no-stick sprays, over time I noticed a crusty build-up that I couldn't remove from my baking tins. I tried scouring with steel wool and scrubbing with an abrasive cleanser. I even tried oven cleaner. Nothing worked. The build-up had become a permanent part of my tins.

My preferred greasing method is to oil the cups using a pastry brush. I pour a little oil into a jar and dip the brush into that. I find the muffins pop out easily and the tins are easy to clean. I use the same brush and oil to coat the top of each muffin after baking (see *Removing Muffins From the Tins* on page 31).

## Filling the Muffin Tins

I fill each cup nearly to the top. The batter should show its head a little above the rim of each cup. This makes for a nice large muffin. Remember that whole-grain muffins do not rise as much as muffins made from refined products. Don't hesitate to fill those tins.

Be sure to fill each cup evenly. If for any reason you do not use all twelve cups, fill the empty cups half-way with water. This allows for even baking of the remaining muffins. Often we want to make exactly the number of muffins that the recipe says to make. But even slight variations in measuring, in the size of muffin tins, or in the way you prepare the batter can change the yield. It is better to fill each baking cup according to the instructions and make one more or one less muffin than to try to ensure that each batch yields exactly twelve muffins.

If you get called away from your muffins right before you are ready to fill the tins—or after you have filled the tins and before you have popped the muffins in the oven—no problem. Muffin batter can sit up to half an hour before baking with no negative consequences. Resist the temptation to stir the batter again. Just spoon it into the tins.

If you have a large oven and plenty of tins, you may want to try this method: Rather than filling every cup in a twelve-muffin tin, fill every other cup with batter. (In this case, you do not need to fill the empty cups with water as previously suggested.) You will use two of the twelve-muffin tins to produce a dozen muffins. This method enhances the quick rising action so necessary for successful muffins.

## Testing for Doneness

When the smell of fresh-baked muffins fills the kitchen, your muffins are done. Yum-O! But let's get down to details. Follow the baking time suggested with each recipe. Press the top of two muffins (on different ends of the tin) to determine doneness. When they spring back, they are done. Timing is a delicate matter. Too much baking yields a dry, hard muffin; too little, a soggy, limp one. Take care. Muffins can fool you. They sometimes look a little soft in the middle and yet they are quite done. It is helpful to remember that muffins continue to cook after you remove them from the oven. Do not overbake.

## Removing Muffins From the Tins

Muffin-making cultivates patience. If you grease the tins generously before baking and allow the muffins to cool at least ten minutes, a gentle twist of the noggin (theirs, not yours) frees them easily from the tins. If you try to force them out of the baking cups before their time, you will need the assistance of a knife or fork or other such implement, and you will cause the muffins to break apart. Plus you run the risk of scratching your tins. Be patient. This step is especially important if you have Teflon coating or other fancy finishes that can be toxic if they are scraped off the tins and consumed.

For added moisture, I brush the top of each muffin with a little oil while the muffins are still nice and hot. The only exception is those muffins that already have a topping.

## Freezing and Reheating

Sometimes I like to bake muffins just for the fun of it and freeze them for later use. Then if there is a last-minute need, or if I get up too late to make a batch for breakfast, I can grab as many muffins as I need and reheat them in a flash.

Muffins are great even after freezing—so long as they are completely cooled before freezing. I freeze them in two ways: I wrap each muffin individually in clear plastic wrap and use a self-adhesive tag to label each one. Or I put four together in a one-quart zip-lock bag and label the bag. I freeze nine to twelve muffins in a gallon-sized zip-lock bag. Stored this way, muffins keep up to three months in the freezer.

To reheat, simply place thawed foil-wrapped muffins in a 400° oven for 5–10 minutes, or place thawed paper-towel-wrapped muffins one at a time in a microwave oven for 10–20 seconds (time varies with each oven). Reheating frozen muffins requires about double these heating times.

## Reviving Day-Old or Older Muffins

You can make day-old muffins taste like fresh-baked by sprinkling them with a little water and warming them. Follow the warming instructions for microwave and conventional ovens (see *Freezing and Reheating* above).

Well, that's about all I have to offer you now. I hope you have found this introduction and the hints useful. Once you discover the natural goodness of my muffins, I know you will want to make them all the time.

# BREAKFAST MUFFINS

*All happiness depends on a leisurely breakfast.*
John Gunther
*Newsweek*

How many times have you heard it said, "Breakfast is the most important meal of the day"? My mom used to tell us to eat breakfast like a king, lunch like a prince, and dinner like a pauper. She said we would be forever healthy.

It made sense to me. But somehow I never quite got the hang of it. I used to get up late, race through a shower, and head for school or the office without breakfast. I'd usually crash by mid morning—often with a thud that could be heard two doors away.

It took me nearly forty years, but I've learned to take mom's advice. For breakfast I eat a fresh-baked, whole-grain muffin—one that will stay with me all morning, supplying much-needed energy as it is slowly digested in my system. When I eat a breakfast muffin, perhaps a bit of fruit or fruit juice, and a cup of coffee, I'm ready for just about anything. And on those days when I have an early morning appetite, I stretch the fare to include eggs or *soysage*. Mmm. Mmm. Mmm. It tastes good. It looks good. I feel good. Heck, I even *look* good.

So what kind of breakfast person are you? Cornmeal mush? Oatmeal and spiced tea? How about blueberries and bran? Or raisins, lots of raisins? Maybe it's something different each day. Whatever the case, I think I've come up with a muffin for you.

P. S. Try as you may, if (despite all your hopes or wishes to the contrary) you inevitably rush out of the house at the last minute, you can still eat healthfully. Muffins are portable. Just toss one in your briefcase, school bag, or back pack and enjoy it later on when you get where you are going.

# Apple-Orange-Oat-Bran Muffins

*I created Apple-Orange-Oat-Bran Muffins for people who want to increase the amount of oat bran in their diets. The orange rind provides a light flavor and the applesauce, a natural sweetness. But feel free to add the optional brown sugar for added flavor and sweetness. Apple-Orange-Oat-Bran Muffins are a crowd-pleasing and nutritious breakfast or snack.*

**Yield:** *12 muffins*

| Dry Ingredients | Wet Ingredients |
| --- | --- |
| 1 1/2 cups unbleached white flour | 1 1/2 cups applesauce |
| 1 cup whole-wheat flour | 1 cup apple juice |
| 2 teaspoons baking powder | 1 teaspoon vanilla extract |
| 1 teaspoon baking soda | 1 tablespoon grated orange rind |
| 1/4 cup brown sugar (optional) | 2 eggs |
| 3/4 teaspoon ground cinnamon | |
| 3/4 teaspoon ground nutmeg | |
| 1 cup oat bran | |

### Goodies

3/4 cup chopped apples (Do not grate.)

1. Preheat oven to 400°.

2. Measure and sift all the dry ingredients *except the oat bran* together in a large bowl. Sift a second time. Add the oat bran and toss to combine. Set aside.

3. Whisk the wet ingredients together in a medium bowl. Add the goodies and stir to combine.

4. Pour the wet ingredients into the dry ingredients. Stir just until mixed. *Do not overstir.*

5. Spoon the batter into greased or papered baking tins. Fill each cup nearly to the top.

6. Bake for 15–20 minutes.

7. Cool in the baking tins for at least 10 minutes. Remove from the tins and brush the top of each muffin with canola oil.

**Serving Suggestions:** Serve with fresh fruit and tea or coffee. Mmm. Mmm. Mmm.

# Blueberry Blintze Muffins

When you go out for breakfast and the menu lists blueberry blintzes, are you inclined to choose them over other selections? Me, too. Blintzes are the kind of treat I just don't make at home. So when I see them at a restaurant, I salivate and place my order.

I created my Blueberry Blintze Muffins to make it easy for me to enjoy the flavors I love, right at home.

Here's a helpful note: Blueberries in muffins have a way of sinking to the bottom and sticking to the tin. It's not the end of the world, but you can avoid this not-so-calamitous-calamity in two ways. First, make sure the batter is nice and thick. That's one thing I like about my Blueberry Blintze Muffins; the ricotta cheese and sour cream make the batter substantial (but not dry) so the fail-safe is written into the recipe. Second, remember that the secret to getting blueberry muffins out of the tins without leaving all the blueberry goodness behind is to cool them a little longer than most muffins—15–20 minutes.

**Yield:** *12 muffins*

| Dry Ingredients | Wet Ingredients |
|---|---|
| 1 cup whole-wheat pastry flour | 3/4 cup ricotta cheese |
| 1 cup whole-wheat flour | 1/2 cup low-fat sour cream |
| 1/4 cup oat flour | 1 cup soy or cow's milk |
| 2 teaspoons baking powder | 1/4 cup canola oil |
| 1 teaspoon baking soda | 1 egg |
| 1/2 teaspoon sea salt | 1/2 cup honey, warmed |
| | 2 teaspoons grated lemon rind |

| Goodies |
|---|
| 1 1/4 cups fresh or frozen blueberries |

1. Preheat oven to 400°.

2. Measure and sift the dry ingredients together in a large bowl. Sift a second time. Set aside.

3. When using fresh berries, wash them first. Remove any stems and leaves. Select 1 1/4 cups of the smallest, firmest berries and add them to the dry ingredients. Toss to coat them with flour. This will keep them from bleeding into the rest of the muffin. (If you are using frozen berries, defrost and drain the berries very well before adding them to the dry ingredients. Discard the liquid.)

4. Whisk the wet ingredients in a medium bowl. *Do not use a blender or food processor.*

5. Pour the wet ingredients into the dry ingredients. Stir just until mixed. *Do not overstir.*

6. Spoon the batter into greased or papered baking tins. Fill each cup nearly to the top.

7. Bake for 15–20 minutes.

8. Cool in the baking tins for at least 15–20 minutes. Remove from the tins and brush the top of each muffin with canola oil.

**Serving Suggestions:** *Blueberry Blintze Muffins* are great with a tall glass of chilled apple juice.

# Blue Morning Muffins

*I value restraint. Once in a while, I think it is good to say, "No. Simply, no!" to those gimme, gimme, gimme thoughts that pop into my head. It helps keep me on my toes, if you know what I mean, and not at the mercy of my impulses.*

*If this is beginning to sound like an apology, it's because it is. You see, what I'm trying to say is that I feel a little guilty for not holding back on the impulse to add coconut to my Blue Morning Muffins—what with the added fat and all. But I think you will agree that the combination of blueberries, blue or yellow cornmeal, and coconut is a great one! If you are on a low-fat diet, eliminate the coconut. The yield of this recipe will be reduced to ten or eleven muffins.*

**Yield:** *12 muffins*

| Dry Ingredients | Wet Ingredients |
|---|---|
| 3/4 cup whole-wheat flour | 1/2 cup applesauce |
| 1 cup unbleached white flour | 1 cup soy or cow's milk |
| 3/4 cup blue or yellow cornmeal | 1/4 cup canola oil |
| 2 teaspoons baking powder | 1 egg |
| 1 teaspoon baking soda | 1/2 cup blueberry or grape |
| 1/2 teaspoon sea salt | all-fruit jam |
| | 1 teaspoon vanilla extract |

**Goodies**

1 1/4 cups fresh or frozen blueberries
3/4 cup coconut (optional)

1. Preheat oven to 375°.

2. Measure and sift the dry ingredients together in a large bowl. Sift a second time. Set aside.

3. Optional: Add the coconut to the dry ingredients and toss.

4. When using fresh berries, wash them first. Remove any stems and leaves. Select 1 1/4 cups of the smallest, firmest berries and add them to the dry ingredients. Toss to coat the berries with flour. This will keep them from bleeding into the rest of the muffin. (If you are using frozen berries, drain the berries very well before adding them to the dry ingredients. Reserve the liquid. If you like, you can substitute 1/4 cup of the reserved liquid for 1/4 cup of the soy or cow's milk. The muffins will be even bluer in the morning!)

5. Whisk the wet ingredients in a small bowl or blend them in your food processor using the purée blade.

6. Pour the wet ingredients into the dry ingredients. Stir just until mixed. *Do not overstir.*

7. Spoon the batter into greased or papered baking tins. Fill each cup nearly to the top.

8. Bake for 15–20 minutes.

9. Cool in the baking tins for at least 15–20 minutes. Remove from the tins and brush the top of each muffin with canola oil.

**Serving suggestions:** Try these with a wedge of cantaloupe.

# Buckwheat (not Farina!) Muffins

One Halloween, my sister Marlene and I dressed up as two of the Little Rascals, Buckwheat and Farina. I remember that I didn't want to be Farina because the name reminded me of that yukky breakfast cereal my dad used to make us eat. I didn't know what buckwheat was, but it had to be better than farina.

Years later, I ordered my first stack of buckwheat pancakes at a breakfast place somewhere in New England. Smothered in about a cup of fresh pure maple syrup . . . you bet, they were better than farina! I've re-created that wonderful combination in my Buckwheat (not Farina!) Muffins. They've got a flavor all their own.

**Yield:** 12 muffins

| Dry Ingredients | Wet Ingredients |
| --- | --- |
| 1 cup whole-wheat pastry flour | 1/2 cup buttermilk |
| 3/4 cup whole-wheat flour | 1/4 cup canola oil |
| 3/4 cup buckwheat flour | 1/4 cup soy margarine or |
| 1 tablespoon baking powder | butter, melted |
| 1/2 teaspoon sea salt | 1 egg |
| | 1 cup maple syrup |

| Goodies |
| --- |
| 1 1/2 cups raisins |

1. Preheat oven to 375°.

2. Measure and sift the dry ingredients together in a large bowl. Sift a second time. Set aside.

3. Whisk the wet ingredients in a small bowl or blend them in your food processor using the purée blade.

4. Add the goodies to the wet ingredients and stir to combine.

5. Pour the wet ingredients into the dry ingredients. Stir just until mixed. *Do not overstir.*

6. Spoon the batter into greased or papered baking tins. Fill each cup nearly to the top.

7. Bake for 15–20 minutes.

8. Cool in the baking tins for at least 10 minutes. Remove from the tins and brush the top of each muffin with canola oil.

***Serving suggestions:*** Serve with a chilled bowl of plain yogurt, sliced peaches, and a cup of black tea.

# California Mix Muffins

*I've never been to California. Can you believe it!? I have planned a coast-to-coast trip no less than four times in my life, and each time, some extenuating circumstance interfered. Once, the person I planned to go with backed out. Once, the van broke down and I missed my "window of opportunity." Once, the trip plan never really got off the ground. And I forget what happened the fourth time.*

*I was beginning to think that the gods were against me. I tried to assuage my disappointment with notions such as, "It's not my destiny," or "I have no karma to work out there," or "I'll get lost in the sea of consciousness." I even tried hating the Californians, "They're all a bunch of cosmic lulus anyway. What do I want with them?" But I wasn't convinced.*

*So I am trying a new tack. I offer my California Mix Muffins on the altar of lost causes and implore the gods for one last chance. By the time this book goes to print, may I walk the sandy beaches of the California coast.*

*P. S. For those who have never heard of it, California mix is the name given to a glorious combination of dried fruits and nuts. It usually contains dried raisins, dates, apricots, pineapple, papaya, and banana, as well as coconut, pumpkin seeds, walnuts, pecans, almonds, and Brazil nuts. Buy it at health-food stores and many commercial markets. California mix often has pieces of dried fruit and nuts that are too large for muffins. You will need to chop it first.*

**Yield:** *10–12 muffins*

| Dry Ingredients | Wet Ingredients |
| --- | --- |
| 2 cups whole-wheat pastry flour | 1 ripe banana (about 1/2 cup) |
| 1/2 cup whole-wheat flour | 1 cup apple juice concentrate |
| 1/2 cup unbleached white flour | 3/4 cup soy or cow's milk |
| 2 teaspoons baking powder | 1/4 cup canola oil |
| 1 teaspoon baking soda | 1 egg |
| | 2 teaspoons vanilla extract |
| | 1 tablespoon grated lemon rind |

---

## Goodies

1 1/2 cups coarsely chopped
California mix

---

1. Preheat oven to 400°.
2. Measure and sift the dry ingredients together in a large bowl. Sift a second time. Set aside.
3. Purée the banana in the food processor using the purée blade. The puréed banana should measure about 1/2 cup. Add the remaining wet ingredients (juice concentrate, milk, oil, egg, extract, and rind) and pulse to blend. (If you do not have a food processor, mash the banana by hand using a fork or potato ricer. Add the remaining wet ingredients and stir to combine.)
4. Add the goodies to the wet ingredients and stir to combine.
5. Pour the wet ingredients into the dry ingredients. Stir just until mixed. *Do not overstir.*
6. Spoon the batter into greased or papered baking tins. Fill each cup nearly to the top.
7. Bake for 15–20 minutes.
8. Cool in the baking tins for at least 10 minutes. Remove from the tins and brush the top of each muffin with canola oil.

*Serving suggestions:* I doubt that you will want to mix up these mixed-up muffins with any other breakfast treat except, perhaps, a nice cup of hot tea.

# Chai Muffins

*Chai is a popular drink in India and Ceylon and at retreat centers and monasteries in the United States and Europe. I first enjoyed it when I took up meditation. Meditators bent on curbing their desire for sensory pleasure (at least during retreat!) had a difficult time when retreat staff served Chai. It is never a one-cup experience—only two or three will do.*

*With my love for spicy cakes and breads, I realized that Chai's exotic blend of spices and tea would make a great muffin. See if you don't agree.*

**Yield:** *12 muffins*

| Goodies | Dry Ingredients |
|---|---|
| 1 3/4 cups water | 1 3/4 cups whole-wheat flour |
| 2 tablespoons grated ginger root | 1 cup unbleached white flour |
| (or 1 tablespoon powdered ginger) | 3/4 cup brown-rice flour |
| 1/4 teaspoon ground anise | 2 teaspoons baking powder |
| 1/4 teaspoon ground cardamom | 1 teaspoon baking soda |
| 1/2 teaspoon ground cinnamon | 1/2 teaspoon sea salt |
| 1/4 teaspoon ground cloves | |
| 2 black tea teabags | |

| Wet Ingredients |
|---|
| 1/4 cup canola oil |
| 1 egg |
| 1/2 cup honey, warmed |

1. Preheat oven to 400°.

2. Bring the water to a boil. Add the ginger root and spices and simmer for about 1/2 hour. The liquid should now measure 1 1/2 cups. If it doesn't, add boiling water to get the right measure. Add the tea and steep for 10 minutes. (Be sure to remove the teabags after 10 minutes.)

3. Add the wet ingredients to the goodies and whisk to combine. Set aside.

4. Measure and sift the dry ingredients together in a large bowl. Sift a second time.

5. Pour the wet ingredients into the dry ingredients. Stir just until mixed. *Do not overstir.*

6. Spoon the batter into greased or papered baking tins. Fill each cup nearly to the top.

7. Bake for 15–20 minutes.

8. Cool in the baking tins for at least 10 minutes. Remove from the tins and brush the top of each muffin with canola oil.

*Serving suggestions:* A cup of plain yogurt is all you need.

# Cornmeal Mush and Seeds Muffins

*I've done a lot of intensive meditation practice in retreat centers and monasteries. The standard breakfast fare in these institutions is hot porridge. Often it is served with such goodies as tahini (puréed sesame seeds), yogurt, honey, bran, nuts, seeds, and dried fruit.*

*I've never been a porridge eater so I thought breakfast would take a little getting used to. But as the retreats progressed and I became more aware of what was happening in my mind and body, I noticed the wonderful warming and nurturing effect of each hot cereal. Rice porridge made me feel nourished but light; oats, warmed and sweet; buckwheat, hot and energized. I noticed that my mind and body were particularly happy when the kitchen staff served up a pot of piping hot cornmeal mush. And with all the interesting goodies to put on top, mush was hard to beat.*

*I tried several combinations of goodies but my favoite was tahini, roasted sunflower seeds, honey, and a sprinkle of cinnamon. And so, the Cornmeal Mush and Seeds Muffins. This is a great recipe for using up leftover cornmeal mush (polenta), or you can make the mush specifically for the muffins.*

**Yield:** *12 muffins*

| Dry Ingredients | Wet Ingredients |
| --- | --- |
| 1 1/2 cups whole-wheat pastry flour | 1/2 cup soy or cow's milk |
| 1/2 cup unbleached flour | 1/4 cup soy margarine or |
| 1 tablespoon baking powder |    butter, melted |
| 1/2 teaspoon ground cinnamon | 1 egg |
| 1 cup coarsely chopped roasted | 1/8 cup honey, warmed |
|    sunflower seeds | |

| Goodies |
| --- |
| scant 1 1/4 cups cornmeal mush (see recipe on page 47) |
| 1/2 cup tahini |

1. Preheat oven to 400°.

2. Measure and sift all the dry ingredients *except the sunflower seeds* together in a large bowl. Sift a second time. Add 1/2 cup of the sunflower seeds to the dry ingredients and toss. Retain 1/2 cup of the seeds to top each muffin. (See step 6 below.)

3. Using the purée blade of your food processor, blend the wet ingredients. Add the goodies and blend again. (If you do not have a food processor, a blender will work just as well.)

4. Pour the wet ingredients into the dry ingredients. Stir just until mixed. *Do not overstir.*

5. Spoon the batter into greased or papered baking tins. Fill each cup nearly to the top.

6. Sprinkle each muffin with 2 teaspoons of the retained chopped sunflower seeds.

7. Bake for 20–25 minutes.

8. Cool in the baking tins for at least 10 minutes.

**Serving suggestions:** If the honey in the muffin isn't enough, drizzle a little more on the finished product! Mmm. Mmm. Mmm.

## Cornmeal Mush

**Yield:** *scant 1 1/4 cups*

1 1/3 cups water                    1/3 cup yellow cornmeal

1. Bring the water to a boil.

2. Slowly pour in the cornmeal while the water is in a rolling boil.

3. Reduce the heat and simmer for 15–20 minutes.

P. S. You can make cornmeal mush the night before and have it ready for the morning's muffins.

# Cracked-Up Wheat Muffins

*Cracked wheat isn't wheat that went crazy. It's raw whole-wheat that was crushed up for you. Isn't that nice and convenient? And it is one of the most nutritious forms of wheat grain.*

*To make this muffin quick and easy, I use bulghur, cracked wheat that has been cooked and dried. Bulghur just needs to be soaked in hot water to become a fluffy wheat delight. To make these muffins sweet, I use apple juice concentrate and dried apples. Dried apples are available at your regular commercial grocery store next to the raisins.*

*Cracked-Up Wheat Muffins are one of the heartiest I make. (The Wheat Berry Surprise Muffins are the heartiest.)*

**Yield:** *12 muffins*

| Goodies | Wet Ingredients |
| --- | --- |
| 2 1/4 cups boiling water | 1 cup apple juice concentrate |
| 1 cup bulghur | 1/4 cup soy margarine or |
| 3/4 cup chopped dried apples |    butter, melted |
| | 1 egg |

| Dry Ingredients | |
| --- | --- |
| 2 cups whole-wheat pastry flour | 1/2 teaspoon sea salt |
| 1/2 cup whole-wheat flour | 1 teaspoon ground cinnamon |
| 1 tablespoon baking powder | |

1. Pour boiling water over the bulghur and dried apples in a medium bowl. Set the bowl aside for 20–30 minutes.

2. Preheat oven to 400°.

3. Measure and sift the dry ingredients together in a large bowl. Sift a second time. Set aside.

4. Whisk the wet ingredients in a small bowl or blend them in your food processor using the purée blade.

5. Combine the wet ingredients with the soaking goodies and stir to combine. Pour the mixture into the dry ingredients. Stir just until mixed. *Do not overstir.*

6. Spoon the batter into greased or papered baking tins. Fill each cup nearly to the top.

7. Bake for 15–20 minutes.

8. Cool in the baking tins for at least 10 minutes. Remove from the tins and brush the top of each muffin with canola oil.


**Serving suggestions:** Try these hot out of the oven with a slice or two of cheese and a fresh apple or pear. Day old, these muffins make great cheese toast for breakfast or for a party hors d'oeuvre. Just cut each muffin into three or four slices and spread the slices on a small baking pan (such as a pie plate or cake tin). Place a slice of your favorite cheese on each muffin, slice, and broil. Mmm, mmm.

# Crazy Raisin Muffins

*Years back, there was a popular raisin cake recipe making the rounds in American kitchens. It called for mayonnaise, lots of raisins, and a hint of cloves. While the raisin part was great, the cake was screaming for more cloves and the mayonnaise had to go (too much cholesterol). Now I've transformed the recipe to make Crazy Raisin Muffins.*

*Just in case your sweet tooth is not quite satisfied with the natural sweetness of raisins, I've added a little honey to the pot. The bears and the bees love it and so do I.*

**Yield:** *12 muffins*

| Goodies | Wet Ingredients |
|---|---|
| 1 cup boiling water | 1 1/2 cups orange juice |
| 2 cups raisins | 1/2 cup soy or cow's milk |
| 1/4 cup honey | 1/4 cup soy margarine or butter, melted |
| | 1 egg |

| Dry Ingredients | |
|---|---|
| 1 1/2 cups whole-wheat pastry flour | 1 teaspoon baking soda |
| 1 cup whole-wheat flour | 1/2 teaspoon sea salt |
| 3/4 cup unbleached white flour | 2 teaspoons ground cloves |
| 2 teaspoons baking powder | 2 teaspoons ground cinnamon |

1. Preheat oven to 400°.

2. Pour the boiling water over the raisins and honey in a medium bowl. Set the bowl aside for 10 minutes while you prepare the remaining ingredients.

3. Measure and sift the dry ingredients together in a large bowl. Sift a second time. Set aside.

4. Whisk the wet ingredients in a small bowl or blend them in your food processor using the purée blade.

5. Add the wet ingredients to the goodies and stir to combine. Pour the mixture into the dry ingredients. Stir just until mixed. *Do not overstir.*

6. Spoon the batter into greased or papered baking tins. Fill each cup nearly to the top.

7. Bake for 15–20 minutes.

8. Cool in the baking tins for at least 10 minutes. Remove from the tins and brush the top of each muffin with canola oil.

*Serving suggestions:* These are extra spicy and outrageous served with cream cheese and a nice hot cup of Earl Grey tea. What a way to start your day!

# Down-to-Earth Date and Nut Muffins

*I must have been Cleopatra in a previous life. I bite into my naturally sweet Down-to-Earth Date and Nut Muffins, close my eyes, and imagine that I am in the the cradle of civilization floating on a barge down the Tigris or Euphrates . . .*

*Okay, so maybe I was only a dock worker who cleaned the barges and fantasized about floating down the river! You know how it is in our reincarnation fantasies; we are always somebody famous or important.*

*Anyway, dates have that ancient quality, don't they? And it's no wonder. Until around the turn of the century when California growers got hip to their commercial value, dates had always been grown almost exclusively in Mesopotamia (or whatever they call that part of the world now).*

*Make it easy on yourself and buy chopped dates.*

**Yield:** *12 muffins*

| Dry Ingredients | Wet Ingredients |
|---|---|
| 1 1/2 cups whole-wheat flour | 1 cup apple juice concentrate |
| 3/4 cup unbleached white flour | 1/2 cup soy or cow's milk |
| 2 tablespoons soy flour | 1/4 cup canola oil |
| 2 teaspoons baking powder | 1 egg |
| 1 teaspoon baking soda | 1/4 cup honey, warmed |
| 1/2 teaspoon sea salt | 1/4 cup molasses, warmed |
| 1 1/2 teaspoons ground cinnamon | |

## Goodies

3/4 cup chopped dates
1 cup coarsely chopped roasted walnuts

1. Preheat oven to 400°.

2. Measure and sift the dry ingredients together in a large bowl. Sift a second time.

3. Add the goodies to the dry ingredients and toss. If the dates are particularly gooey, be sure to break them into bits and coat the bits with the flour, or you will get clumps of dates unevenly situated throughout the muffins.

4. Whisk the wet ingredients in a small bowl or blend them in your food processor using the purée blade.

5. Pour the wet ingredients into the dry ingredients. Stir just until mixed. *Do not overstir.*

6. Spoon the batter into greased or papered baking tins. Fill each cup nearly to the top.

7. Bake for 15–20 minutes.

8. Cool in the baking tins for at least 10 minutes. Remove from the tins and brush the top of each muffin with canola oil.

**Serving suggestions:** Do I need to tell you how to enjoy *Down-to-Earth Date and Nut Muffins?* With *cream cheese!!!* And dates are so naturally sweet, you do not need to top these muffins with any other sweetener.

# Eat-Your-Oatmeal Muffins

My current favorite breakfast cereal is creamy oatmeal with a hint of spice and topped with chopped fruit, nuts, and raisins. Can you blame me for wanting to make a muffin that captures all these flavors in one?

With this recipe, I recommend using fresh apples or pears. These fruits are almost always available and they hold up beautifully in muffins. You needn't peel the fruit. Just scrub, core, and quarter. Then either chop by hand or use your food processor.

Eat-Your-Oatmeal Muffins are a favorite with children, for breakfast or anytime. They taste like a great big oatmeal cookie.

**Yield:** *12 muffins*

| Dry Ingredients | Wet Ingredients |
|---|---|
| 2 cups whole-wheat pastry flour | 1/2 cup apple juice concetrate |
| 1 1/4 cups rolled oats | 3/4 cup soy or cow's milk |
| 2 teaspoons baking powder | 1/4 cup canola oil |
| 1 teaspoon baking soda | 1 egg |
| 1/2 teaspoon sea salt | 1/4 cup honey, warmed |
| 1 teaspoon ground cinnamon | 1 1/2 teaspoons vanilla extract |
| 3/4 teaspoon powdered ginger | |

| Goodies |
|---|
| 1 1/4 cups chopped apples and/or pears (Do not grate.) |
| 1/2 cup raisins |
| 1/2 cup roasted sunflower seeds |

1. Preheat oven to 400°.

2. Measure and sift the dry ingredients together in a large bowl. Sift a second time. Set aside.

3. Add the goodies to the dry ingredients and toss.

4. Whisk the wet ingredients in a small bowl or blend them in your food processor using the purée blade.

5. Pour the wet ingredients into the dry ingredients. Stir just until mixed. *Do not overstir.*

6. Let the batter stand for about 5 minutes before spooning it into the baking tins. (The oatmeal needs to absorb some moisture from the batter before baking.)

7. Spoon the batter into greased or papered baking tins. Fill each cup nearly to the top.

8. Bake for 15–20 minutes.

9. Cool in the baking tins for at least 10 minutes. Remove from the tins and brush the top of each muffin with canola oil.


**Serving suggestions:** Try these with *Peanut Butter and Apple Butter Spread* (see *Gloria's Glorious Muffin Butters and Spreads* on page 56).

# Gloria's Glorious Muffin Butters and Spreads

## Apple Butter Spread
**Yield:** 3/4 cup
Cream* 4 ounces cream cheese
with 1/4 cup apple butter
and 1 teaspoon grated ginger root
(or 1/2 teaspoon powdered ginger).

## Chocolate/Peanut Butter Spread
**Yield:** 3/4 cup
Blend* 1/2 cup smooth peanut butter,
2 tablespoons cocoa,
1 tablespoon canola oil,
and 1/4 cup honey.

## Honey/Cinnamon Spread
**Yield:** 1/2 cup
Cream* 1/2 cup soy margarine or butter
with 1 tablespoon honey
and 1/2 teaspoon ground cinnamon.

## Maple Butter
**Yield:** 1/2 cup
Cream* 1/2 cup soy margarine or butter
with 6 tablespoons pure maple syrup.

# Lemon Spread

**Yield:** 1/2 cup

Cream* 1/2 cup soy margarine, butter, or cream cheese
with 3 tablespoons lemon juice,
4 tablespoons rice syrup,
or 2 tablespoons honey, warmed,
and 1 teaspoon finely grated lemon rind.

# Peanut Butter and Apple Butter Spread

**Yield:** 3/4 cup

Blend* 1/4 cup smooth peanut butter,
with 1/2 cup apple butter.

# Sweety/Fruity Spread

**Yield:** 1 cup

Cream* 1/2 cup soy margarine or butter
with 1/2 cup all-fruit jam, jelly, or marmalade
and 1/2 teaspoon lemon rind.

*Use a hand-held mixer to blend or cream all muffin butters and spreads or blend or cream them by hand. Do not use a blender or food processor.

# Fakin' Bacon Muffins

*Fakin' bacon is a scrumptious way to enjoy the smoked flavor of bacon with none of the cholesterol, a fraction of the fat, about half the sodium, and, of course, no meat. Because it is made from tempeh (a cultured soy bean and/or grain product that is a popular source of protein for vegetarians), it is chock-full of protein goodness. Look for it in your local health-food store under a variety of names.*

*The name fakin' bacon implies that it is imitation bacon. I prefer to think of it as* real *smoked tempeh. If you haven't tried it, there's no time but the present.*

**Yield:** *10 muffins*

| Goodies | Wet Ingredients |
| --- | --- |
| 6–8-ounce package fakin' bacon | 2 cups soy or cow's milk |
| 1 tablespoon canola oil | 1/4 cup canola oil |
| 1/4 cup chopped onion (optional) | 1 egg |

| Dry Ingredients | |
| --- | --- |
| 1 cup whole-wheat flour | 1/4 cup millet flour |
| 1 3/4 cups unbleached white flour | 1 tablespoon baking powder |

1. Using a medium skillet, crumble and sauté the fakin' bacon in 1 tablespoon canola oil until it is lightly browned. Remove the fakin' bacon from the skillet; drain well on a paper towel to remove the excess oil.

2. Preheat oven to 400°.

3. Measure and sift the dry ingredients together in a large bowl. Sift a second time. Set aside.

4. Add the fakin' bacon to the dry ingredients and toss to coat with flour. If necessary, crumble large chunks of fakin' bacon.

5. Optional: Add the onion to the dry ingredients and toss.

6. Whisk the wet ingredients in a small bowl or blend them in your food processor using the purée blade.

7. Pour the wet ingredients into the dry ingredients. Stir just until mixed. *Do not overstir.*

8. Spoon the batter into greased or papered baking tins. Fill each cup nearly to the top.

9. Bake for 15–20 minutes.

10. Cool in the baking tins for at least 10 minutes. Remove from the tins and brush the top of each muffin with canola oil.

**Serving suggestions:** *Fakin' Bacon Muffins* are great with eggs (what else?), any style.

# Glazed Sunrise Blueberry Muffins

*When I watch the sun come up—or when I eat one of my Glazed Sunrise Blueberry Muffins—I am reminded of a poem by Oliver Wendell Holmes:*

*The morning light, which rains its quivering beams*
*Wide o'er the plains, the summits, and the streams,*
*In one broad blaze expands its golden flow*
*On all that answers to its glance below.*

*I dreamed up this recipe when I was making the Very Berry Bran Muffins (page 88) because I think citrus and blueberries are a great combination for a breakfast muffin and a wonderful way to "answer to the glance" of sunrise. To my way of thinking, the glaze adds an extra burst of sunshine. See if you don't agree.*

**Yield:** *12 muffins*

| Dry Ingredients | Wet Ingredients |
|---|---|
| 1 1/2 cups unbleached white flour | 1 cup lemon juice or orange juice |
| 1 1/2 cups whole-wheat pastry flour | 1 cup soy or cow's milk |
| 2 teaspoons baking powder | 1/2 cup soy margarine or |
| 1 teaspoon baking soda |    butter, melted |
| 1/2 teaspoon sea salt | 1 egg |
| | 1/2 cup honey, warmed |
| | 3 tablespoons grated lemon |
| |    or orange rind |

### Goodies

1 1/4 cups fresh or frozen blueberries

## Topping

*Citrus Honey Glaze* (see *Gloria's Glorious Glazes* on page 168.)

1. Preheat oven to 375°.

2. Measure and sift the dry ingredients together in a large bowl. Sift a second time. Set aside.

3. When using fresh berries, wash them first. Remove any stems and leaves. Select 1 1/4 cups of the smallest, firmest berries and add them to the dry ingredients. Toss to coat them with flour. This will keep them from bleeding into the rest of the muffin. (If you are using frozen berries, defrost and drain the berries very well before adding them to the dry ingredients. Discard the liquid.)

4. Whisk the wet ingredients in a small bowl or blend them in your food processor using the purée blade.

5. Pour the wet ingredients into the dry ingredients. Stir just until mixed. *Do not overstir.*

6. Spoon the batter into greased or papered baking tins. Fill each cup nearly to the top.

7. Bake for 15–20 minutes.

8. Topping: While the mufins bake, prepare the *Citrus Honey Glaze*.

9. When the muffins are done, cool them for about 15–20 minutes in the baking tins. Remove from the tins and coat each muffin with enough glaze to cover the top surface. Cool for an additional 10 minutes before you dig in.

**Serving suggestions:** Try making these with different combinations and permutations of citrus. Try lemon juice with orange rind, or orange juice with lemon rind, or all orange, or all lemon, or orange with lemon glaze, or lemon with orange glaze . . . You get the picture.

# Gloria's Granola Muffins

In my twenties, I lived in a van and travelled up and down the East Coast, whistle-stopping at my friends' homes and visiting places I had always wanted to see. I had a small cooler that I rarely filled with ice, and a Coleman stove that never seemed to have any gas. Given my limited kitchen facilities, granola with powdered milk or fruit juice was my staple. I found it nutritious enough to keep me healthy and delicious enough to eat every day without tiring of it. What a life!

Whenever I had access to a kitchen, I'd make a gallon or two of granola, which I stored in air-tight plastic jars. To this day I still make my own (see recipe for Homemade Granola on page 64).

If you don't make your own granola, you can buy a commercial brand at health-food stores, food co-ops, and open-air markets. Today's granola comes in all shapes, sizes, and flavors—almond, apple, maple, orange, and even blueberry and raspberry. You can make Gloria's Granola Muffins with any flavor granola you like.

*Yield: 12 muffins*

| Goodies | Wet Ingredients |
| --- | --- |
| 1 1/2 cups granola | 1/4 cup canola oil |
| 3/4 cup apple juice | 1 egg |
| 3/4 cup soy or cow's milk | 1/2 cup all-fruit orange marmalade |
| | 1–2 teaspoons grated orange rind |

| Dry Ingredients | |
| --- | --- |
| 1 1/4 cups whole-wheat pastry flour | 1 teaspoon baking soda |
| 1 cup whole-wheat flour | 1/4 teaspoon sea salt |
| 3/8 cup oat flour | 3/4 teaspoon ground cinnamon |
| 2 teaspoons baking powder | 3/4 teaspoon ground nutmeg |

1. Combine the goodies in a medium bowl. Let stand for about 10 minutes.

2. Preheat oven to 400°.

3. Measure and sift the dry ingredients together in a large bowl. Sift a second time. Set aside.

4. Whisk the wet ingredients in a medium bowl or blend them in your food processor using the purée blade. Add the wet ingredients to the goodies and stir to combine.

5. Pour the wet ingredients into the dry ingredients. Stir just until mixed. *Do not overstir.*

6. Spoon the batter into greased or papered baking tins. Fill each cup nearly to the top.

7. Bake for 15–20 minutes.

8. Cool in the baking tins for at least 10 minutes. Remove from the tins and brush the top of each muffin with canola oil.

*Serving Suggestions:* For a nutritious and delicious breakfast, try *Gloria's Granola Muffins* with orange marmalade (all-fruit marmalade, of course) and fresh grapefruit. And while you are at it, how about a cup of English Breakfast (Assam) tea?

# Homemade Granola

*Yield: 8–10 cups*

| Dry Ingredients | Wet Ingredients |
| --- | --- |
| 5 cups oats | 1/2 cup honey, warmed * |
| 1/2 cup oat or wheat bran | 1/2 cup canola oil |
| 1 cup raw wheat germ | 2 teaspoons grated orange rind |
| 1/2 cup soy flour | 1 teaspoon vanilla extract |
| 1 cup sunflower seeds | |
| 1/2 cup sesame seeds | |
| 1/2 teaspoon salt | |

### Goodies

1 cup each dried bananas, raspberries, blueberries, roasted almonds, raisins, dates, and/or coconut

1. Combine the dry ingredients in a large bowl. Mix well.

2. Combine the wet ingredients in a small bowl and stir well.

3. Pour the wet ingredients over the dry ingredients and mix to coat.

4. Spread the mixture on a cookie sheet and toast it in a pre-heated 300°F oven for 40–45 minutes, stirring every 15 minutes.

5. Cool for about 15 minutes then crumble as you like it—fine or chunky.

6. After crumbling the granola, add 1 cup each of your favorite flavors such as dried bananas, dried raspberries, dried blueberries, roasted almonds, raisins and/or dates, or coconut. Use any combination and any amount of the above.

*If you like a maple-flavored granola, substitute 1 cup of maple syrup for the honey and add 1 cup of chopped walnuts after the granola cools.

# Irish Soda Muffins

My sister Betty makes Irish soda bread whenever the family gets together. One of the selling features in a houseful of calorie-counters is that the bread contains no sugar! I adapted this recipe from her age-old bread recipe. Okay, so I added a little melted butter to make it rich. But if you are concerned about the added saturated fat, use 1/4 cup more canola oil instead.

Irish Soda Muffins have an unforgettable taste. They are unusual enough that they come to mind when I ask myself, "What could I have for breakfast that's really interesting?" Yet, they are ordinary enough that I always seem to have the ingredients on hand. And Irish Soda Muffins are probably the most versatile muffin I make—lending themselves well to any meal, any time of day. See if you don't agree that they are a real attention-getter.

**Yield:** *12 muffins*

| Goodies | Wet Ingredients |
|---|---|
| 3 tablespoons hot water | 2 cups buttermilk |
| 1 1/2 cups raisins | 1/4 cup canola oil |
| 3 tablespoons grated orange rind | 1/4 cup soy margarine or |
| 2 tablespoons caraway seeds |   butter, melted |
| | 1 egg |

| Dry Ingredients | |
|---|---|
| 1 1/2 cups whole-wheat pastry flour | 1 1/2 teaspoons baking powder |
| 1 cup whole-wheat flour | 1 teaspoon baking soda |
| 1/2 cup unbleached white flour | 1/4 teaspoon sea salt |

1. Preheat oven to 400°.

2. Combine the goodies in a medium bowl. Set aside.

3. Measure and sift the dry ingredients together in a large bowl. Sift a second time. Set aside.

4. Whisk the wet ingredients in a small bowl or blend them in your food processor using the purée blade. Add the wet ingredients to the goodies and stir to combine.

5. Pour the wet ingredients into the dry ingredients. Stir just until mixed. *Do not overstir.*

6. Spoon the batter into greased or papered baking tins. Fill each cup nearly to the top.

7. Bake for 15–20 minutes.

8. Cool in the baking tins for at least 10 minutes. Remove from the tins and brush the top of each muffin with canola oil.


***Serving suggestions:*** I cut my *Irish Soda Muffins* in half, place the bottom half in a bowl, and crack a three-minute boiled egg on top. Then I enjoy the top half of the muffin with a smidgeon of all-fruit jam. You will not believe this combination!

# Jewish Mother Muffins

*Potato latkes are wonderful potato pancakes that are usually made with grated potatoes, egg, flour, and milk and served with applesauce and sour cream. They are a popular menu item at Jewish delis and restaurants and have always been a favorite of mine. I especially like them for breakfast because they are like a cross between pancakes and home-fried potatoes, two of my favorite breakfast treats.*

*To capture the wonderful potato flavor of latkes, I use instant potato flakes in my Jewish Mother Muffins. Potato flakes are dehydrated potatoes that have been chipped into a light and flaky powder. You can buy them in health-food stores or your regular grocery. I have noticed that the brands sold at the health-food stores are especially nutritious because they have been made from the whole potato—skins and all. The skins contain most of the potato nutrients. Look for potato flakes that actually are flakes. If you buy instant potatoes that have the consistency of a fine powder rather than a flake, your muffins will turn out dense and heavy.*

**Yield:** *12 muffins*

| Goodies | Wet Ingredients |
| --- | --- |
| 1/2 cup boiling water | 1 1/2 cups soy or cow's milk |
| 1 cup chopped dried apples | 3/4 cup low-fat sour cream |
| 1 tablespoon canola oil | 1/4 cup soy margarine or |
| 1/2 package fakin' bacon |    butter, melted |
|    (3–4 ounces) | 1 egg |
| 1/4 cup chopped onion | |
| 1 cup instant potato flakes | |
| 1 tablespoon chopped chives | |

| Dry Ingredients | |
| --- | --- |
| 1 1/2 cups whole-wheat pastry flour | 1 tablespoon baking powder |
| 1/2 cup unbleached white flour | 1 teaspoon sea salt |

1. Pour the boiling water over the chopped dried apples in a medium bowl. Set the bowl aside while you prepare the remaining ingredients.

2. Using a small skillet, crumble and sauté the fakin' bacon in 1 tablespoon canola oil until it is lightly browned. Remove the fakin' bacon from the skillet; drain well on a paper towel to remove the excess oil. Set aside.

3. Preheat oven to 400°.

4. Measure and sift the dry ingredients together in a large bowl. Sift a second time. Set aside.

5. Whisk the wet ingredients in a medium bowl or blend them in your food processor using the purée blade.

6. Add all the goody ingredients (the soaked dried apples, the cooked fakin' bacon, the onion, potato flakes, and chives) to the wet ingredients. Stir to evenly distribute the goodies throughout.

7. Pour the wet ingredients into the dry ingredients. Stir just until mixed. *Do not overstir.*

8. Spoon the batter into greased or papered baking tins. Fill each cup nearly to the top.

9. Bake for 20–25 minutes.

10. Cool in the baking tins for at least 10 minutes. Remove from the tins and brush the top of each muffin with canola oil.

**Serving suggestions:** These muffins make a great breakfast treat with fried eggs or all alone.

# Ladda's Lemon Ginger Muffins

*Ladda is a Thai woman that I met at a Buddhist monastery in England. Every Sunday, she'd arrive at the monastery before mealtime and brew a huge pot of lemon ginger tea. She'd mash about four roots of ginger into a stringy pulp and boil them in five or six gallons of water. Then she'd add about a dozen sliced lemons, an ounce or two of crumbled chrysanthemum leaves and a pound of raw sugar. The tea would simmer for about an hour while everyone waited in patient Buddhist style.*

*The ginger gives the tea a bite that warms all the way down and has a pacifying effect on the internal organs. And the aroma! We drank the tea all afternoon while we learned about the Buddhist teachings from the monks and nuns. Then we'd offer them a flask to take back to their rooms (and we'd fill a flask for ourselves, too!) so the tea could continue to do its magic into the cold English night.*

*I created Ladda's Lemon Ginger Muffins as a tribute to Ladda and the warmth she shared.*

**Yield:** *12 muffins*

| Dry Ingredients | Wet Ingredients |
| --- | --- |
| 1 1/2 cups whole-wheat flour | 3/4 cup lemon juice |
| 1 1/2 cups unbleached white flour | 1 cup soy or cow's milk |
| 2 tablespoons soy flour | 1/4 cup canola oil |
| 2 teaspoons baking powder | 1 egg |
| 1 teaspoon baking soda | 1/2 cup honey, warmed |
| 1/2 teaspoon sea salt | |
| 1/2 teaspoon ground coriander | |

## Goodies

2 tablespoons grated ginger root
  (or 1 tablespoon powdered ginger)
3 1/2 tablespoons grated lemon rind

1. Preheat oven to 375°.

2. Measure and sift the dry ingredients together in a large bowl. Sift a second time. Set aside.

3. Whisk the wet ingredients in a small bowl or blend them in your food processor using the purée blade.

4. Combine the goodies with the wet ingredients and stir well.

5. Pour the wet ingredients into the dry ingredients. Stir just until mixed. *Do not overstir.*

6. Spoon the batter into greased or papered baking tins. Fill each cup nearly to the top.

7. Bake for 15–20 minutes.

8. Cool in the baking tins for at least 10 minutes. Remove from the tins and brush the top of each muffin with canola oil.

*Serving suggestions:* For an interesting change, try substituting orange rind and orange juice for the lemon rind and lemon juice. These are such nice muffins to pop into your mouth that I often make them into mini-muffins. This recipe yields 36 mini-muffins; bake them for 10–15 minutes.

# Maple Pecan Muffins

*I like to go out for breakfast on Saturday mornings with my friends Donna and Cashin. We go to what must be the most unassuming restaurant in America. Everything is served up hot and home style. Don't look for any fancy garnishes or mood music. This place is only a step up from an interstate truck stop.*

*I never need to look at the menu because I know exactly what I want—pecan waffles with maple syrup. These have a flavor unlike any other waffles I've tasted. One morning, Donna asked what distinguishes these waffles from the pack. The waitress told us they put malt powder in the batter.*

*My Maple Pecan Muffins bring forth that same wonderful flavor. I use a generous measure of malted milk powder, and I've taken it a step further by using barley flour as well. You see, malt powder is derived from sprouted barley that has been toasted and ground to a powder. The barley flour adds another touch of wonderful barley nut goodness.*

**Yield:** *12 muffins*

| Dry Ingredients | Wet Ingredients |
| --- | --- |
| 1 cup whole-wheat pastry flour | 3/4 cup soy or cow's milk |
| 1/2 cup unbleached white flour | 1/4 cup soy margarine or |
| 3/4 cup barley flour | butter, melted |
| 1 tablespoon baking powder | 1 egg |
| 1/2 teaspoon sea salt | 1 cup maple syrup |

| Goodies |
| --- |
| 1 1/2 cups coarsely chopped roasted pecans |
| 1/2 cup malted milk powder |

BREAKFAST MUFFINS

1. Preheat oven to 400°.
2. Measure and sift the dry ingredients together in a large bowl. Sift a second time.
3. Add the goodies to the dry ingredients and toss. Set aside.
4. Whisk the wet ingredients in a small bowl or blend them in your food processor using the purée blade.
5. Pour the wet ingredients into the dry ingredients. Stir just until mixed. *Do not overstir.*
6. Spoon the batter into greased or papered baking tins. Fill each cup nearly to the top.
7. Bake for 15–20 minutes.
8. Cool in the baking tins for at least 10 minutes. Remove from the tins and brush the top of each muffin with canola oil.

**Serving suggestions:** If these don't have enough maple flavor to suit your palate, you may want to mix up some *Maple Butter* (see *Gloria's Glorious Muffin Butters and Spreads* on page 56).

# Marvelous Marmalade Crumb Muffins

*In an article in* Town and Country *magazine, Jeanine Larmoth wrote, "Marmalade in the morning has the same effect on the taste buds that a cold shower has on the body." Isn't it the truth? The tastebuds wake up from a deep slumber with a smile on their faces.*

*These muffins will make you smile for sure. You loved jelly donuts when you were a kid. Now you can enjoy a nutritious muffin with marmalade filling and a light coffeecake crumble topping. If the grownups get their hands on these first, there will be none left for the kids!*

*If you have a favorite all-fruit jelly or jam, use it instead of marmalade. Then you can call these Jimdandy Jelly Crumb Muffins!*

**Yield:** *12 muffins*

| Topping | Wet Ingredients |
|---|---|
| 1/4 cup Sucanat or brown sugar | 3/4 cup apple juice concentrate |
| 1/2 cup whole-wheat pastry flour | 1/2 cup soy or cow's milk |
| 1/2 cup unbleached white flour | 1/2 cup all-fruit marmalade, |
| 1/4 cup soy margarine or butter |    jelly, or jam |
|    (softened to room temperature) | 1/4 cup canola oil |
| | 1 egg |

| Dry Ingredients | |
|---|---|
| 1 cup whole-wheat flour | 2 teaspoons baking powder |
| 1 cup unbleached white flour | 1/2 teaspoon baking soda |
| 1/2 cup barley flour | 1/4 teaspoon sea salt |

# BREAKFAST MUFFINS

## Goodies

1/2 cup all-fruit marmalade, jelly, or jam (approximate)

1. Topping: To make the topping, combine the Sucanat or brown sugar and flour in a medium bowl. Using a pastry blender or two knives, cut the butter or soy margarine into the flour and Sucanat or brown sugar to form a crumbly topping. Set aside.

2. Preheat oven to 375°.

3. Measure and sift the dry ingredients together in a large bowl. Sift a second time. Set aside.

4. Whisk the wet ingredients in a small bowl or blend them in your food processor using the purée blade.

5. Pour the wet ingredients into the dry ingredients. Stir just until mixed. *Do not overstir.*

6. Spoon half the batter into greased or papered baking tins. Then measure 1 level teaspoon of marmalade onto the batter in the center of each cup. Spoon the remaining batter into the baking cups, taking care to enclose the marmalade in the center of the batter.

7. Spoon 2 teaspoons of crumb topping on each muffin.

8. Bake for 15–20 minutes.

9. Cool in the baking tins for at least 10 minutes.

*Serving suggestions: Marvelous Marmalade Crumb Muffins* cry out for coffee, coffee, coffee!

# Peanut-Butter Rice-Cake Muffins

*Rice cakes are a rather benign food—so benign as to be uninteresting—pockets of air with the occasional vein of puffed rice. It wasn't until someone introduced me to rice cakes smothered with peanut butter, sliced bananas, raisins, sunflower seeds, a drizzle of honey, and a sprinkle of cinnamon that I truly learned to appreciate rice cakes—probably because I couldn't taste them; I could only hear them crunch.*

*I use rice syrup in these muffins for the wonderful flavor and the added nutrition. However, rice syrup is quite expensive. You can substitute 1/4 cup of warmed honey plus 1/4 cup soy or cow's milk for the rice syrup in this recipe.*

**Yield:** *12 muffins*

| Dry Ingredients | Wet Ingredients |
| --- | --- |
| 1/2 cup whole-wheat pastry flour | 2 cups mashed ripe bananas |
| 1/2 cup whole-wheat flour | (about 4 whole) |
| 1/2 cup unbleached white flour | 1/4 cup soy or cow's milk |
| 1/2 cup brown-rice flour | 1/2 cup chunky peanut butter |
| 1 tablespoon baking powder | 1/4 cup canola oil |
| 1/2 teaspoon sea salt | 1/2 cup rice syrup, warmed |
| 3/4 teaspoon ground cinnamon | |

| Goodies |
| --- |
| 1 cup raisins |
| 1 cup roasted sunflower seeds |

1. Preheat oven to 375°.

2. Measure and sift the dry ingredients together in a large bowl. Sift a second time. Set aside.

3. Purée the bananas in the food processor using the purée blade. The puréed banana should measure about 2 cups. Add the remaining wet ingredients (milk, peanut butter, oil, and rice syrup) and pulse to blend. (If you do not use a food processor, mash the banana by hand using a fork or potato ricer. Add the remaining wet ingredients and stir to combine.)

4. Combine the goodies with the wet ingredients and stir to combine. Pour the mixture into the dry ingredients. Stir just until mixed. *Do not overstir.*

5. Spoon the batter into greased or papered baking tins. Fill each cup nearly to the top.

6. Bake for 15–20 minutes.

7. Cool in the baking tins for at least 10 minutes. Remove from the tins and brush the top of each muffin with canola oil.

**Serving suggestions:** Slice *Peanut-Butter Rice-Cake Muffins* and serve them with a tall glass of apple or cranberry juice.

# Proof-of-the-Pudding Muffins

When I practice meditation at Buddhist monasteries and retreat centers, I pay a lot of attention to food. In an environment where most sensual pleasures are deliberately removed, mealtime can assume paramount importance!

Once each month, a generous staff-member at one of the retreat centers I visited rose three hours before breakfast to bake Indian pudding for the hundred or so meditators. I was so grateful to her and used to count the days until it was time for Indian pudding to be served again. I'd ask myself, "What is it about Indian pudding that makes me so happy?" Ginger knocks me out, it's true. And not enough good things can be said about cinnamon. But there is something very earthy about the combination of cornmeal, milk, eggs, and molasses. Cervantes said, "The proof of the pudding is in the eating." Never was this more true than with Indian pudding. I loved the pudding then and I love it now—especially if there happens to be some dried fruit to add to it!

I created my Proof-of-the-Pudding Muffins to capture the wonderful combination of spices and sweetener that I enjoy in Indian pudding.

**Yield:** *12 muffins*

| Dry Ingredients | Wet Ingredients |
| --- | --- |
| 2 cups whole-wheat pastry flour | 1 3/4 cups soy or cow's milk |
| 1/2 cup unbleached white flour | 1/4 cup soy margarine or |
| 1 cup yellow cornmeal | butter, melted |
| 2 teaspoons baking powder | 1 egg |
| 1 teaspoon baking soda | 1/4 cup molasses, warmed |
| 1/2 teaspoon sea salt | 1/2 teaspoon vanilla extract |
| 1 teaspoon ground cinnamon | |
| 1/2 teaspoon ground nutmeg | |

## Goodies

3/4 cup raisins

2 tablespoons grated ginger root
  (or 1 tablespoon powdered ginger)

2 teaspoons grated orange rind

1. Preheat oven to 400°.

2. Measure and sift the dry ingredients together in a large bowl. Sift a second time. Set aside.

3. Whisk the wet ingredients together in a small bowl or blend them in your food processor using the purée blade.

4. Add the goodies to the wet ingredients. Stir to combine.

5. Pour the wet ingredients into the dry ingredients. Stir just until mixed. *Do not overstir.*

6. Spoon the batter into greased or papered baking tins. Fill each cup nearly to the top.

7. Bake for 15–20 minutes.

8. Cool in the baking tins for at least 10 minutes. Remove from the tins and brush the top of each muffin with canola oil.

**Serving suggestions:** Top *Proof-of-the-Pudding Muffins* with whipped butter or a smear of low-fat sour cream.

# Soysage Cheese Muffins

A popular party hors d'oeuvre in the South is sausage cheese balls—little biscuit-like puffs of bleached white flour made with hot pork sausage and cheddar cheese. I first tasted them at a political function back in 1984. I didn't want to be rude to my hostess so I accepted her invitation to taste one, despite the ingredients. I had to admit, the flavor was appealing, but knowing how unwholesome they were, I couldn't bring myself to go back for more.

When I started making muffins, I decided to re-create the appealing hors d'oeuvre's flavor using soysage (a soybean product that tastes like sausage but is all vegetable) and extra sharp cheddar cheese.

There are a number of soysage products on the market—from links, to patties, to bulk packets. People's tastes vary, so I suggest that you try a few brands to see which one you like best. You want to end up with about 1 cup of browned ground soysage that resembles ground beef in texture and appearance.

**Yield:** 12 muffins

| Goodies | Wet Ingredients |
|---|---|
| 1/4 pound hot spicy soysage | 1 cup buttermilk |
| 1 tablespoon canola oil | 1 cup soy or cow's milk |
| 1 cup grated extra sharp | 1/4 cup canola oil |
| cheddar cheese | 2 eggs |
| 1/4 teaspoon cayenne pepper (optional) | |

| Dry Ingredients | |
|---|---|
| 1 cup whole-wheat flour | 1/2 teaspoon sea salt |
| 1 cup unbleached white flour | 1/8 teaspoon pepper |
| 1/2 cup amaranth flour | 1 teaspoon rubbed sage |
| 1 tablespoon baking powder | |

1. Using a medium skillet, crumble and sauté the soysage in 1 tablespoon canola oil until it is lightly browned. Remove the soysage from the skillet, drain well on a paper towel to remove the excess oil, and place it in the medium bowl. Add the remaining goodie ingredients (grated cheese and optional cayenne pepper) and toss.

2. Preheat oven to 400°.

3. Measure and sift the dry ingredients together in a large bowl. Sift a second time.

4. Add the goodies to the dry ingredients and toss to coat with flour. If necessary, crumble large chunks of soysage.

5. Whisk the wet ingredients in a small bowl or blend them in your food processor using the purée blade.

6. Pour the wet ingredients into the dry ingredients. Stir just until mixed. *Do not overstir.*

7. Spoon the batter into greased or papered baking tins. Fill each cup nearly to the top.

8. Bake for 15–20 minutes.

9. Cool in the baking tins for at least 10 minutes. Remove from the tins and brush the top of each muffin with canola oil.

*Serving suggestions:* I think you will agree that these are great for the mornings when you want something hot and spicy for breakfast. Or you can serve mini-muffins at your next political function! This recipe yields 36 mini-muffins; bake them for 10–15 minutes.

# Start-a-Movement Muffins

*You say you haven't made a decent visit in three days . . .*
*You say you're so backed up that every time you bend over you burp . . .*
*You say you've tried everything from salt water, to bran cakes, to "Professor Ehret's*
*Mucusless Fat-Free Diet Healing System" and you're still about to bust . . .*
*Is that's what's bothering you, friend?*

*Well, step right up and discover the amazing powers of prunes and bran*
*together for the first time in Gloria's Glorious Start-a-Movement Muffins. If*
*these don't do the job, nothing will.*

*Take these muffins along to keep you regular when you travel to new places.*
*But you must promise me one thing. Promise me that you won't eat more than*
*one? Three prunes have more fiber than one bowl of bran flakes—and these*
*muffins contain both!*

**Yield:** *12 muffins*

| Dry Ingredients | Wet Ingredients |
| --- | --- |
| 1 3/4 cups whole-wheat pastry flour | 1 1/2 cups apple juice |
| 1 cup unbleached white flour | 1/2 cup soy or cow's milk |
| 2 teaspoons baking powder | 1/4 cup canola oil |
| 1 teaspoon baking soda | 1 egg |
| 1/2 teaspoon sea salt | 1/4 cup molasses, warmed |
| 1 teaspoon ground cinnamon | 2 teaspoons grated orange rind |
| 1/2 cup wheat bran | |

### Goodies

1 1/2 cups coarsely chopped pitted prunes (about 24)

1. Preheat oven to 400°.

2. Measure and sift all the dry ingredients *except the wheat bran* together in a large bowl. Sift a second time. Add the wheat bran and toss. Set aside.

3. Add the goodies to the dry ingredients and toss. If the prunes are particularly gooey, be sure to break them into bits and coat the bits with the flour, or you will get clumps of prunes unevenly situated throughout the muffins.

4. Whisk the wet ingredients in a small bowl or blend them in your food processor using the purée blade.

5. Pour the wet ingredients into the dry ingredients. Stir just until mixed. *Do not overstir.*

6. Spoon the batter into greased or papered baking tins. Fill each cup nearly to the top.

7. Bake for 15–20 minutes.

8. Cool in the baking tins for at least 10 minutes. Remove from the tins and brush the top of each muffin with canola oil.

*Serving suggestions:* Chase these with a glass of chilled prune juice. Ha! Ha! Only kidding.

# Sunny Banana Bran Muffins

Bananas are so great. It makes me giggle just thinking about them. But have you ever had banana anything that had enough banana in it? Me either. That is, not until I created my Sunny Banana Bran Muffins—three whole cups of mashed ripe bananas. That's about six bananas in twelve muffins. Go for it!

Oh, I like mine spicy. If you prefer pure banana flavor, forget the cinnamon and nutmeg.

Knowing when your bananas are ready for use in baking can be a delicate matter. As bananas ripen, they get brown specks on the skin. When overripe, they are completely brown. You want them when they are past "just ripe" and not quite overripe. At this point, I think they are sweet without being too sweet, and moist without being gooey.

Often you can buy ripe bananas at the grocery store at reduced prices. Go ahead and buy them even if you are not ready to use them in muffins. You can mash the bananas and freeze them in plastic containers until you are ready to bake.

P. S. Did you know that the banana is a berry, the largest on earth?

**Yield:** 12 muffins

| Dry Ingredients | Wet Ingredients |
| --- | --- |
| 1 cup whole-wheat pastry flour | 3 cups mashed ripe bananas |
| 1 cup whole-wheat flour | (about 6 whole) |
| 1/2 cup unbleached white flour | 1/2 cup canola oil |
| 1 cup wheat bran | 1 egg |
| 2 1/2 teaspoons baking powder | 1/4 cup honey, warmed |
| 1/2 teaspoon baking soda | 3/4 teaspoon vanilla extract |
| 3/4 teaspoon ground cinnamon | 1 teaspoon grated lemon rind |
| 3/4 teaspoon ground nutmeg | |
| 1 cup roasted sunflower seeds | |

1. Preheat oven to 375°.

2. Measure and sift all the dry ingredients *except the sunflower seeds* together in a large bowl. Sift a second time. Add the sunflower seeds and toss. Set aside.

3. Purée the bananas in the food processor using the purée blade. The puréed banana should measure about 3 cups. Add the remaining wet ingredients (oil, egg, honey, extract, and rind) and pulse to blend. (If you do not use a food processor, mash the banana by hand using a fork or potato ricer. Add the remaining wet ingredients and stir to combine.)

4. Pour the wet ingredients into the dry ingredients. Stir just until mixed. *Do not overstir.*

5. Spoon the batter into greased or papered baking tins. Fill each cup nearly to the top.

6. Bake for 15–20 minutes.

7. Cool in the baking tins for at least 10 minutes. Remove from the tins and brush the top of each muffin with canola oil.

*Serving suggestions:* Want to be totally outrageous? Spread a little *Chocolate/Peanut Butter Spread* (see *Gloria's Glorious Muffin Butters and Spreads* on page 56) on your *Sunny Banana Bran Muffins*. Mmm, mmmm, mmmm!

# Thanks-to-the-Tropical-Sun Muffins

In American restaurants when you order fruit cup for breakfast, you get anything from tinned fruit cocktail to nicely prepared fresh fruit in season, depending upon the quality of the restaurant you frequent. Despite the wide range in quality, American restaurants seem to agree upon one thing—fresh fruit servings are itsie, bitsie, teenie, weenie.

You can imagine my surprise when I ordered fresh fruit at a lovely little waterfront restaurant in Veracruz, Mexico, and the waiter brought me a meat platter full of sliced mango, papaya, and other tropical delights! It was enough to feed four people! And, I might add, it was the most memorable serving of fruit I have ever eaten.

Here's to that restaurant in Veracruz—whatever its name—and here's to the tropical sun that made these wonderful fruits possible.

P. S. My Peachy Peach Muffins on page 184 are a variation on Thanks-to-the-Tropical-Sun Muffins but are made with ingredients that are more readily available. Try those, too.

**Yield:** *12 muffins*

| Dry Ingredients | Wet Ingredients |
|---|---|
| 3/4 cup whole-wheat flour | 1/2 cup canola oil |
| 1 cup whole-wheat pastry flour | 1 egg |
| 1 cup unbleached white flour | 1/2 cup peach or apricot |
| 2 teaspoons baking powder | all-fruit jam |
| 1 teaspoon baking soda | 1 teaspoon rum extract |
| 1/2 teaspoon sea salt | 1 teaspoon grated lemon rind |

## Goodies

1 1/2 cups fresh mango or a 1-pound
    can of mango packed in fruit juice
1 cup chopped dried papaya

1. Preheat oven to 400°.
2. Measure and sift the dry ingredients together in a large bowl. Sift a second time. Set aside.
3. Whisk the wet ingredients in a medium bowl or blend them in your food processor using the purée blade and place them in a medium bowl.
4. Using the purée blade of your food processor, purée the fresh or canned mango. (If you do not have a food processor, mash the mango by hand using a fork or a potato ricer.) Measure and add the puréed mango to the wet ingredients. Add the remaining goody ingredient (dried papaya) and stir to combine.
5. Pour the wet ingredients into the dry ingredients. Stir just until mixed. *Do not overstir.*
6. Spoon the batter into greased or papered baking tins. Fill each cup nearly to the top.
7. Bake for 15–20 minutes.
8. Cool in the baking tins for at least 10 minutes. Remove from the tins and brush the top of each muffin with canola oil.

**Serving suggestions:** Keep up the tropical spirit with slices of fresh banana, pineapple, or mango. Trust me. It won't be too much fruit.

# Very Berry Bran Muffins

*What's a muffin cookbook without a berry muffin recipe? Right? And what's a berry muffin without bran? Mmm. Mmm. As much as I love my other breakfast muffins, I have to admit that I make these most frequently. My friends tell me they are among my best.*

*I think fresh blueberries and raspberries work best with these muffins, but I also make them with cranberries. If you use cranberries, soak them in an additional 1/4 cup of warmed honey for about 15 minutes before you begin.*

*I realize you can't always get fresh berries. If you make these muffins with frozen berries, drain the berries very well before adding them to the dry ingredients. If you like, you can substitute up to 1/4 cup of the drained liquid for an equal amount of apple juice. Just be warned that your Very Berry Bran Muffins will be very berry blue or red.*

**Yield:** *12 muffins*

| Dry Ingredients | Wet Ingredients |
| --- | --- |
| 1 1/4 cups whole-wheat pastry flour | 1 3/4 cups apple juice |
| 1 1/4 cups whole-wheat flour | 1/4 cup canola oil |
| 2 teaspoons baking powder | 1 egg |
| 1 teaspoon baking soda | 1/2 cup honey, warmed |
| 1/2 teaspoon sea salt | 3/4 teaspoon vanilla extract |
| 3/4 teaspoon ground cinnamon | 1 teaspoon grated lemon rind |
| 3/4 teaspoon ground nutmeg | |
| 1 cup wheat bran | |

| Goodies |
| --- |
| 1 1/4 cups fresh or frozen berries |

1. Preheat oven to 375°.

2. Measure and sift all the dry ingredients *except the wheat bran* together in a large bowl. Sift a second time. Add the wheat bran and toss. Set aside.

3. Wash the berries. Remove any stems and leaves. Select 1 1/4 cups of the smallest, firmest berries and add them to the dry ingredients. Toss to coat them with flour. This keeps them from bleeding into the rest of the muffin. (If you are using frozen berries, drain the berries very well before adding them to the dry ingredients. If you like, you can substitute 1/4 cup of the drained liquid for 1/4 cup of the the apple juice.)

4. Whisk the wet ingredients in a small bowl or blend them in your food processor using the purée blade.

5. Pour the wet ingredients into the dry ingredients. Stir just until mixed. *Do not overstir.*

6. Spoon the batter into greased or papered baking tins. Fill each cup nearly to the top.

7. Bake for 15–20 minutes.

8. Cool in the baking tins for at least 15–20 minutes. Remove from the tins and brush the top of each muffin with canola oil.

**Serving suggestions:** Try these with *Lemon Spread* or *Sweety/Fruity Spread* (see *Gloria's Glorious Muffin Butters and Spreads* on page 57) and a slice of cantaloupe.

# Wheat Berry Surprise Muffins

Made with seven grains and whole-wheat berries, these are the heartiest muffins in the lot. My intention with Wheat Berry Surprise Muffins was to create a no-frills multigrain muffin that stands on its own two feet—one that is great with just about anything.

For an added treat, try lightly toasting the flour first. Measure and sift the required amounts of flour. Place half in a large skillet over a medium flame and toast for a few minutes (until the flour barely begins to brown and you can smell the aroma). Remove the flour from the heat and place it in a large bowl. Repeat with the remaining flour. Cool to room temperature before making the muffins.

**Yield:** 16 muffins

| Goodies | Wet Ingredients |
|---|---|
| 1/3 cup wheat berries | 1 3/4 cups soy or cow's milk |
| 1 cup boiling water | 1/2 cup canola oil |
| | 1 egg |
| | 1/2 cup less 1 tablespoon honey, warmed |
| | 1 tablespoon molasses, warmed |
| | 2 teaspoons grated lemon rind |

| Dry Ingredients | |
|---|---|
| 1 3/4 cups whole-wheat pastry flour | 1/4 cup millet flour |
| 1/4 cup amaranth flour | 2 teaspoons baking powder |
| 1/2 cup rye flour | 1 teaspoon baking soda |
| 1/4 cup brown-rice flour | 1/2 teaspoon sea salt |
| 1/4 cup barley flour | 1/4 cup rolled oats |

1. Cook the wheat berries as follows: Rinse the 1/3 cup of wheat berries in cold water. Add them to the 1 cup boiling water. Reduce heat and simmer for about 1/2 hour until berries are soft. They should be the consistency of cooked brown rice. Remove berries from heat and set aside. (*Note:* You can cook the wheat berries the night before and store them overnight in the refrigerator.)

2. Preheat oven to 400°.

3. Measure and sift all the dry ingredients *except the rolled oats* together in a large bowl. Sift a second time. Add the rolled oats and toss. Set aside.

4. Whisk the wet ingredients in a small bowl or blend them in your food processor using the purée blade.

5. Combine the cooked wheat berries with the wet ingredients and stir. Pour the mixture into the dry ingredients. Stir just until mixed. *Do not overstir.*

6. Spoon the batter into greased or papered baking tins. Fill each cup nearly to the top.

7. Bake for 15–20 minutes.

8. Cool in the baking tins for at least 10 minutes. Remove from the tins and brush the top of each muffin with canola oil.


**Serving suggestions:** Try *Wheat Berry Surprise Muffins* for breakfast hot out of the oven, or enjoy them with a tossed salad for lunch. They are especially great with eggs (any style), honeydew melon, and strawberries.

# SAVORY/DINNER
# MUFFINS

*For a man seldom thinks with more earnestness*
*of anything than he does his dinner.*

Samuel Johnson

I like my life to be coordinated. When I wear a pink T-shirt, I want to wear pink socks, not yellow. When I eat Chinese food, I want a fortune cookie or almond cookie for dessert, not New York cheesecake. You know what I mean? That's why I wrote this chapter of *Gloria's Glorious Muffins*. With *Savory/Dinner Muffins*, you can bake muffins to match any cuisine—from the simplest to the most gourmet—and provide a memorable accompaniment to your meal at the same time. In fact, with *Savory/Dinner Muffins* you can *create* the cuisine—Italian, French, Chinese, Japanese, Indian, Middle Eastern, Jewish, Mexican, and good old American. Just add a salad and a simple bowl of soup and, presto . . . an unforgettable meal.

Lately, I've taken to inviting friends over for lunch instead of going out. What we do is simple. Someone brings a salad, another a soup, and I prepare a batch of muffins. It costs each of us very little money and is so much nicer than dining out. The meal is hearty and stays with us all afternoon, thus diminishing the likelihood that we will want a big dinner.

Or what about this scenario . . . You've prepared a meal that doesn't come out quite as you had hoped or wished or wanted. You may have spent hours in the kitchen putting together your best Indian banquet only to have it taste, well, mediocre. At the last minute, you can pizazz it up with *Chutney* or *Cashew Curry Muffins*. The muffins will be so gratifying that people won't notice that the rest of the meal fell a little short of your expectations.

P.S. I use vegetable broth in many of the muffins in this chapter to give them added flavor and nutrition. Make it easy on yourself by buying powdered vegetable boullion at your local health-food store. The boullion mixes with water and adds wholesome vegetable flavor without a lot of fuss and muss.

# Artichoke Hearts Muffins

*Remember your first artichoke? Who can forget it. Your host or hostess hands you a plate with an oversized army-green pine cone resting pertly atop a bed of red-leaf lettuce, and enthusiastically invites you to dig in. Not wanting to appear ungrateful, you respond with a lively "Oh, boy!"—all the while wondering how on earth you are going to tackle the thorny object before you. "What am I supposed to do with that?" you whisper softly to yourself. "Make a Christmas wreath?"*

*Minutes later, having followed the lead of the other guests, you find your taste buds are doing trampoline flips inside your mouth as you scrape and suck every morsel of flesh from each succulent leaf—all the while noticing that the deeper into the artichoke you go, the sweeter it gets. "May I please have another cup of garlic/lemon butter dip," you babble, hoping no one will notice the dribble running over the top of your lower lip.*

*And just when you think that this delectable experience is drawing to a close, you discover that the best of the artichoke is before you—an exquisite, tender heart. You ask yourself, "Where have I been all my life?"*

*I believe you will agree that I have done justice to this wonder with my Artichoke Hearts Muffins.*

**Yield:** *12 muffins*

| Dry Ingredients | Wet Ingredients |
| --- | --- |
| 2 cups whole-wheat pastry flour | 1 1/2 cups vegetable broth |
| 1/2 cup unbleached white flour | 1/4 cup olive oil |
| 1/2 cup millet flour | 1 egg |
| 1 tablespoon baking powder | |
| 1 teaspoon sea salt | |
| 1/4 teaspoon ground black pepper | |

## Goodies

| | |
|---|---|
| 4 whole artichoke hearts, canned in water (approximate) | 1 teaspoon crumbled dried rosemary |
| | 1 teaspoon dried basil |
| 1/2 cup grated romano cheese | 1 clove minced garlic |

1. Preheat oven to 400°.

2. Measure and sift the dry ingredients together in a large bowl. Sift a second time. Set aside.

3. Whisk the wet ingredients in a medium bowl or blend them in your food processor using the purée blade and pour them into a medium bowl.

4. Using the purée blade of your food processor, prepare the goodies as follows: Quarter the artichoke hearts and place them in your food processor. (Add enough hearts to yield 3/4 cup.) Add the remaining goodie ingredients (cheese, rosemary, basil, and garlic). Pulse a few times to chop and blend. Add the mixture to the wet ingredients. Stir to combine. (If you do not have a food processor, chop the hearts by hand. Add the hearts and remaining goodie ingredients to the wet ingredients, and stir to combine.)

5. Pour the wet ingredients into the dry ingredients. Stir just until mixed. *Do not overstir.*

6. Spoon the batter into greased or papered baking tins. Fill each cup nearly to the top.

7. Bake for 15–20 minutes.

8. Cool in the baking tins for at least 10 minutes. Remove from the tins and brush the top of each muffin with olive oil.

*Serving suggestions:* Try these with tomato and black olive salad.

# Barley Mushroom Muffins

*There are times in nearly all our lives when money gets scarce and we find ourselves searching for inventive ways to eat well on a strict budget. When I need to tighten my purse strings, I always seem to rediscover a hearty soup made with whole-grain barley, carrots, and mushrooms. It is inexpensive, nutritious, and tastes so delicious that I enjoy it by candlelight.*

*Like that soup, my Barley Mushroom Muffins are good for the heart, easy on the purse, and delightful to the palate. You can buy nutritional yeast flakes at your health-food store. Be sure you are buying nutritional yeast flakes and not brewer's yeast. Okay?*

*P. S. If you have never cooked with nutritional yeast flakes, you are in for a taste treat. My love affair with nutritional yeast began several years ago when I first used it in a gravy. I was delighted to find a gravy for my mashed potatoes that could be made exclusively from vegetable products . . . What can I say? Nutritional yeast flakes have one of those tastes I cannot describe. You'll just have to sample it for yourself. So, try it, you'll like it!*

**Yield:** *10 muffins*

| Goodies | Dry Ingredients |
|---|---|
| 2/3 cup water | 1 cup whole-wheat pastry flour |
| 1/3 cup whole-grain barley | 1/2 cup whole-wheat flour |
| 1 1/4 cups chopped mushrooms | 1/2 cup unbleached white flour |
| 2 tablespoons chopped onion | 1/2 cup barley flour |
| 1/4 cup grated carrot | 1 tablespoon baking powder |
| 1 teaspoon dried basil | 1/4 teaspoon ground black pepper |
| | 2 tablespoons nutritional yeast flakes |

## Wet Ingredients

| | |
|---|---|
| 1 cup vegetable broth | 1 egg |
| 1/2 cup soy or cow's milk | 1/4 cup soy sauce |
| 1/4 cup olive oil | |

1. Cook the barley as follows: Bring 2/3 cup of water to a boil. Add 1/3 cup of whole-grain barley, cover, and simmer for 20 minutes or until the barley is soft. The cooked barley should measure 1 cup. Set aside.

2. Preheat oven to 400°.

3. Measure and sift all the dry ingredients *except the nutritional yeast flakes* together in a large bowl. Sift a second time. Add the nutritional yeast flakes and toss. Set aside.

4. Whisk the wet ingredients in a medium bowl or blend them in your food processor using the purée blade and pour them into a medium bowl.

5. Add the cooked barley and the remaining goodie ingredients (mushrooms, onion, carrots, basil) to the wet ingredients. Stir to combine.

6. Pour the wet ingredients into the dry ingredients. Stir just until mixed. *Do not overstir.*

7. Spoon the batter into greased or papered baking tins. Fill each cup nearly to the top.

8. Bake for 20–25 minutes.

9. Cool in the baking tins for at least 10 minutes. Remove from the tins and brush the top of each muffin with olive oil.

*Serving suggestions:* Try these by candlelight.

# Bearnaise Muffins

*I can't remember the last time I had bearnaise sauce. It was probably the last time I had filet mignon. I miss it—the bearnaise, that is. It's not as if I lie awake nights, moaning in anguish. It's more as if the thought of bearnaise sauce makes me smile with fond memories.*

*Since I've gotten away from red meat, I haven't really found the right vegetarian dish for bearnaise sauce. I invented Bearnaise Muffins to bring the sauce back into my life—and yours.*

**Yield:** *10 muffins*

| Dry Ingredients | Goodies |
|---|---|
| 3 cups whole-wheat pastry flour | 2 teaspoons chopped onion |
| 1/2 cup unbleached white flour | 1 tablespoon soy sauce |
| 1 tablespoon baking powder | 2 teaspoons dijon mustard |
| 1/2 teaspoon baking soda | 1 1/2 tablespoons dried tarragon |
| 1/4 teaspoon ground pepper | 1 tablespoon chopped chives |

| Wet Ingredients | |
|---|---|
| 1 cup vegetable broth | 1/4 cup soy or cow's milk |
| 1/4 cup lemon juice | 1/4 cup olive oil |
| 1/4 cup cooking sherry | 1 egg |

1. Preheat oven to 400°.

2. Measure and sift the dry ingredients together in a large bowl. Sift a second time. Set aside.

3. Whisk the wet ingredients in a small bowl or blend them in your food processor using the purée blade.

4. Add the goodies to the wet ingredients and stir to combine.

5. Pour the wet ingredients into the dry ingredients. Stir just until mixed. *Do not overstir.*

6. Spoon the batter into greased or papered baking tins. Fill each cup nearly to the top.

7. Bake for 15–20 minutes.

8. Cool in the baking tins for at least 10 minutes. Remove from the tins and brush the top of each muffin with olive oil.

**Serving suggestions:** *Bearnaise Muffins* go great with cream of asparagus soup or miso broth and a nice garden salad.

# Brazilian Black-Bean Muffins

*From time to time, I go on a black-bean binge. I don't know what causes it. Does anybody know how these things happen? I like to think that my body needs black beans, and every now and then it sends a signal from some sensory receptor, through a series of synaptic connections, to my memory banks, and into my conscious mind. "Black beans. Black beans. Give this body black beans."*

*That's what I like to think. But more than likely, someone mentions black beans in passing, or I smell something that reminds me of black beans, or an image of black beans comes into my mind. Then I salivate and go into a piggy feeding-frenzie as I frantically check the bean cupboard. That's the way it is with me and black beans so it is no surprise that I turned my favorite black-bean soup recipe into Brazilian Black-Bean Muffins. They'll satisfy any black-bean feeding-frenzie.*

**Yield:** *12 muffins*

| Dry Ingredients | Wet Ingredients |
|---|---|
| 1 cup whole-wheat pastry flour | 1 cup vegetable broth |
| 1 1/2 cups whole-wheat flour | 1/4 cup orange juice |
| 1/2 cup unbleached white flour | 1/4 cup low-fat sour cream |
| 1 tablespoon baking powder | 1 egg (optional) * |
| 1/4 teaspoon pepper | |

| Goodies | |
|---|---|
| 1 1/2 cups canned or home-cooked black beans, well drained | 1 tablespoon ground cumin |
| | 1 teaspoon ground coriander |
| 1/2 cup liquid from the beans | 1 teaspoon celery seed |
| 2 cloves minced garlic | 3 tablespoons cooking sherry |
| 2 tablespoons soy sauce | |

1. Preheat oven to 400°.

2. Measure and sift the dry ingredients together in a large bowl. Sift a second time. Set aside.

3. Drain the beans, reserving 1/2 cup of liquid. Rinse the beans under cold water. Add the beans, reserved liquid, and the remaining goodie ingredients (garlic, soy sauce, cumin, coriander, celery seed, and sherry) to the food processor and purée. (If you do not have a food processor, a blender will work just as well for steps 3 and 4. However, you may need to blend the goodies and wet ingredients together at the same time in order to have sufficient moisture to purée the beans.) Remove the goodies from the processor and place them in a medium bowl.

4. Using the purée blade of your food processor, blend the wet ingredients. Add the wet ingredients to the goodies and stir to a smooth consistency.

5. Pour the wet ingredients into the dry ingredients. Stir just until mixed. *Do not overstir.*

6. Spoon the batter into greased or papered baking tins. Fill each cup nearly to the top.

7. Bake for 15–20 minutes.

8. Cool in the baking tins for at least 10 minutes. Remove from the tins and brush the top of each muffin with canola oil.

*Serving suggestions:* Remember what I said about a meal in a muffin? That's what these are. Try them with a cup of vegetable broth and a garden salad with feta cheese.

---

\* The beans act as a binding agent so if you're restricting your egg consumption, you need not use an egg to hold these muffins together.

# Brie-with-Brandy Muffins

*My friend Steven throws the best parties. What makes them wonderful is the fabulous array of hors d'oeuvres he offers his guests. His brie-with-brandy spread has become one of my all-time favorites. I shared the recipe with my friend Nancy, and I noticed that she has made it one of her standbys as well. It has such a delicious combination of flavors that it was destined to become a muffin.*

*And these muffins have a golden goody in them—golden raisins. When sulfur dioxide gas is used to dry grapes, they retain their natural golden color. Drying grapes in this way also helps retain vitamin C. While sulfur dioxide is on the Generally Recognized As Safe (GRAS) list of the United States Food and Drug Administration, some people prefer not to eat foods dried in this way. If you are such a person, make these with regular dark raisins.*

**Yield:** *12 muffins*

| Dry Ingredients | Wet Ingredients |
| --- | --- |
| 3 cups whole-wheat pastry flour | 8-ounce wheel of brie cheese |
| 1/2 cup unbleached white flour | 1 1/4 cups soy or cow's milk |
| 1 tablespoon baking powder | 1/2 cup canola oil |
| 1/2 teaspoon baking soda | 1 egg |
| 1/2 teaspoon sea salt | 2 teaspoons brandy extract |

### Goodies

1/4 cup Sucanat or brown sugar
1 cup golden raisins
1 1/2 cups slivered almonds

1. Preheat oven to 400°.

2. Measure and sift the dry ingredients together in a large bowl. Sift a second time. Set aside.

3. Using a medium saucepan over medium heat, melt the brie together with the soy or cow's milk. Remove from heat.

4. Using the purée blade of your food processor, blend the brie mixture along with the remaining wet ingredients (oil, egg, and extract) to a smooth consistency. (If you do not have a food processor, use a blender to blend the ingredients.) Pour the mixture into a medium bowl.

5. Add the Sucanat or brown sugar, raisins, and 1 1/8 cups of slivered almonds to the wet ingredients and stir to combine. Retain the remaining 3/8 cup of slivered almonds to top each muffin (see step 8).

6. Pour the wet ingredients into the dry ingredients. Stir just until mixed. *Do not overstir.*

7. Spoon the batter into greased or papered baking tins. Fill each cup nearly to the top.

8. Top each muffin with approximately 1 teaspoon slivered almonds.

9. Bake for 15–20 minutes.


**Serving suggestions:** *Brie-with-Brandy Muffins* make an amazing meal served with sliced fruit and tea. They are also sweet enough to serve for dessert (with sliced apples!).

# Cashew Curry Muffins

*Ever since I began cooking for myself, curried anything has been a favorite meal of mine. But it wasn't until recent years that I learned there are as many blends of curry powder as there are uses for it! And now I've added one more use—muffins!*

*Curry is usually prepared from any or all of the following: allspice, cayenne, cardamom, coriander, cloves, cumin, fennel, fenugreek, garlic, ginger, mace, mustard, pepper, poppy seed, and tumeric—with coriander and tumeric being the most dominant ingredients. Depending on the particular combination of spices, curry powder can range from dark brown, to bright orange, to amber gold, to mellow yellow in color, inexpensive to exorbitant in cost, and mild to three-alarm-fire in taste. It has a depth and intensity that is unmatched by any other combination of spices.*

*If you are familiar with a number of curry powders or make your own, choose the one that you like best for Cashew Curry Muffins. Any blend will provide a mouth-watering muffin.*

**Yield:** *12 muffins*

| Dry Ingredients | Wet Ingredients |
| --- | --- |
| 2 cups whole-wheat pastry flour | 1 1/4 cups vegetable broth |
| 1/2 cup unbleached white flour | 1/4 cup lemon juice |
| 2 teaspoons baking powder | 1/4 cup olive oil |
| 1/2 teaspoon baking soda | 1 egg |
| 1/2 teaspoon sea salt | |
| 2 tablespoons curry powder | |
| 2 tablespoons Sucanat or | |
|    brown sugar | |

## Goodies

| | |
|---|---|
| 1 1/2 cups coarsely chopped roasted cashews | 2 cloves minced garlic |
| | 1 tablespoon grated ginger root |
| 1 cup chopped apples (*Do not grate.*) | (or 1 1/2 teaspoons powdered ginger) |
| 3/4 cup raisins | 1/2 cup flaked coconut (optional) |

1. Preheat oven to 400°.

2. Measure and sift the dry ingredients together in a large bowl. Sift a second time. Set aside.

3. Whisk the wet ingredients in a medium bowl or blend them in your food processor using the purée blade and place them in a medium bowl.

4. Add 1 1/8 cups of the cashews to the wet ingredients. Retain the remaining 3/8 cup to top each muffin (see step 7). Add the remaining goody ingredients (apples, raisins, garlic, ginger, and optional coconut) to the wet ingredients and stir to combine.

5. Pour the wet ingredients into the dry ingredients. Stir just until mixed. *Do not overstir.*

6. Spoon the batter into greased or papered baking tins. Fill each cup nearly to the top.

7. Top each muffin with approximately 1 1/2 teaspoons chopped cashews.

8. Bake for 15–20 minutes.

9. Cool in the baking tins for at least 10 minutes.

*Serving suggestions:* Cashew Curry Muffins go great with stir-fry veggies and rice, with hard-boiled eggs and fresh garden salad, or with a bowl of carrot or tomato soup.

# Chili Beanie Muffins

*I spent a couple of months in Mexico, travelling around the Yucatan Peninsula and visiting the archaeological ruins. When I first arrived, my travel companion, a Mexican, offered me an egg sandwich with what he considered to be a "reasonable" portion of jalapeño peppers. Having no reason to doubt his judgement, I chomped into the fare. "Yeow!" I screamed, spitting jalapeños everywhere, "Is that what you call 'reasonable'?"*

*By the end of my stay, I noticed that I had acquired such an affection for the teary-eyed, sniffly-nosed charge I got from eating jalapeños that my sandwiches had noticeably more peppers than anything else! I've been similarly generous with the hot stuff in my Chili Beanie Muffins. If they are too hot for you, cut back on the cayenne pepper and jalapeños.*

*P. S. Make it easy on yourself. Buy the black olives and jalapeño peppers already chopped.*

**Yield:** *12 muffins*

## Dry Ingredients

| | |
|---|---|
| 1 1/2 cups whole-wheat flour | 1 teaspoon baking soda |
| 1 cup unbleached white flour | 1 teaspoon sea salt |
| 1/2 cup yellow cornmeal | 1/4 teaspoon pepper |
| 2 teaspoons baking powder | |

## Goodies

| | |
|---|---|
| 1 cup canned or home-cooked red kidney beans, well drained | 2 cloves minced garlic |
| | 1 tablespoon chili powder |
| 1/2 cup liquid from the beans | 1 teaspoon dried basil |
| 4 -ounce can of chopped black olives | 2 teaspoons dried oregano |
| 4 -ounce can of chopped jalapeño peppers, well drained | 1 tablespoon dried parsley |
| | scant 1/2 teaspoon cayenne pepper |

## Wet Ingredients

1/4 cup lemon juice

1 1/4 cups tomato juice

1/4 cup canola oil

1 egg (optional) *

1. Preheat oven to 400°.

2. Measure and sift the dry ingredients together in a large bowl. Sift a second time. Set aside.

3. Drain the beans, reserving 1/2 cup of liquid. Rinse the beans under cold water. Add the beans, reserved liquid, and the remaining goody ingredients (olives, peppers, garlic, chili powder, basil, oregano, parsley, and cayenne) to the food processor and purée. Remove the goodies from the processor and place them in a medium bowl. (If you do not have a food processor, a blender will work just as well.)

4. Using the purée blade of your food processor, blend the wet ingredients. (If you do not have a food processor, a blender will work just as well.) Add the wet ingredients to the goodies and stir to a smooth consistency.

5. Pour the wet ingredients into the dry ingredients. Stir just until mixed. *Do not overstir.*

6. Spoon the batter into greased or papered baking tins. Fill each cup nearly to the top.

7. Bake for 20–25 minutes.

8. Cool in the baking tins for at least 10 minutes. Remove from the tins and brush the top of each muffin with canola oil.

*Serving suggestions:* Serve these with sliced Monterrey jack cheese and a glass of chilled water!

---

* The beans act as a binding agent so if you're restricting your egg consumption, you need not use an egg to hold these muffins together.

# Chutney Muffins

Chutney is a delectable relish-y condiment made from fresh fruits, dried fruits, sweetener, vinegar, and spices. It is a common accompaniment for curried dishes. In fact, these dishes are not the same without chutney.

Most commercial brands of chutney, while they may be delicious, are made with refined sugar, and they are quite expensive. I like to make my own chutney because it is less expensive and I am able to improvise recipes to eliminate the sugar. In addition, I find I am able to produce a wider variety of flavors than if I limited myself to store-bought chutney. You see, you can make chutney from fresh fruits such as apples, apricots, mango, peaches, and pineapple, and from many dried fruits. As you can imagine, each type of chutney has its own distinct flavor. Check through your cookbooks for interesting chutney recipes and try them with my Chutney Muffins.

Whether you use a store-bought brand or make your own chutney, take care when making these muffins. After it has been chopped, the 1 3/4 cups of chutney that you use in this recipe should have the texture of relish. If yours is dry, add enough water to get the desired consistency. If it's runny, eliminate some of the vegetable broth in this recipe.

**Yield:** *10 muffins*

| Dry Ingredients | Wet Ingredients |
| --- | --- |
| 3 cups whole-wheat pastry flour | 3/4 cup vegetable broth |
| 1/2 cup unbleached white flour | 1/4 cup canola oil |
| 2 tablespoons soy flour | 1 egg |
| 1 tablespoon baking powder | |

| Goodies |
| --- |
| 1 3/4 cups coarsley chopped chutney |

1. Preheat oven to 400°.

2. Measure and sift the dry ingredients together in a large bowl. Sift a second time. Set aside.

3. Whisk the wet ingredients together in a medium bowl or blend them in your food processor using the purée blade and pour them into a medium bowl.

4. Add the chopped chutney to the wet ingredients. Stir to combine.

5. Pour the wet ingredients into the dry ingredients. Stir just until mixed. *Do not overstir.*

6. Spoon the batter into greased or papered baking tins. Fill each cup nearly to the top.

7. Bake for 15–20 minutes.

8. Cool in the baking tins for at least 10 minutes. Remove from the tins and brush the top of each muffin with canola oil.

***Serving suggestions:*** I created my *Chutney Muffins* to accompany my favorite Indian meals, but they go well with Middle Eastern and Chinese cuisines, too.

# Cosmic Cottage Dill Muffins

My sister Diane is the inspiration behind these muffins. Twenty years ago when I was a freshman in college, I made her a loaf of cottage dill bread. She hasn't given me a moment's peace since then. Quite naturally, when I told her about my idea for a muffin cookbook, she said I had to include a cottage dill muffin. She was right. These are truly cosmic.

Now when I visit my sister, I make her a couple of dozen muffins with the idea that she and her family should eat one dozen and freeze the second. The second dozen rarely makes it to the freezer.

**Yield:** *12 muffins*

| Dry Ingredients | Wet Ingredients |
| --- | --- |
| 1 3/4 cups whole-wheat flour | 1 cup low-fat cottage cheese |
| 1 3/4 cups unbleached white flour | 1 1/2 cups soy or cow's milk |
| 2 tablespoons wheat or oat bran | 1/4 cup canola oil |
| 1 tablespoon baking powder | 1 egg |
| 1/2 teaspoon sea salt | 1 tablespoon honey |

| Goodies |
| --- |
| 2 tablespoons chopped onion |
| 2 tablespoons dill seeds |

1. Preheat oven to 400°.

2. Measure and sift the dry ingredients together in a large bowl. Sift a second time. Set aside.

3. Whisk the wet ingredients in a medium bowl. *Do not use a blender or food processor.*

4. Add the goodies to the wet ingredients and stir to combine.

5. Pour the wet ingredients into the dry ingredients. Stir just until mixed. *Do not overstir.*

6. Spoon the batter into greased or papered baking tins. Fill each cup nearly to the top.

7. Bake for 15–20 minutes.

8. Cool in the baking tins for at least 10 minutes. Remove from the tins and brush the top of each muffin with canola oil.

**Serving suggestions:** *Cosmic Cottage Dill Muffins* are great for any meal but go especially well with simple vegetable or egg dishes. Try them with an egg omelet or a slice of quiche with fruit. Mmm. Mmm! Mmm!

# Cucci Cucci Couscous Muffins

*During the late sixies, I stumbled upon a wonderful recipe for tabouli (a Middle Eastern wheat salad made from bulghur, sliced tomato, lemon, parsley, and a refreshing hint of mint). Health-food stores of the day were in the habit of printing recipes on tear-off cards strategically tacked alongside the various products they hoped to sell. The idea was to offer a recipe and serving suggestions to fledgling natural foods enthusiasts. It was quite the fashion and very helpful, I thought. Anyway, I dutifully helped myself to the recipe card for tabouli, and have held on to it all these years, making only slight modifications. It serves as the basis for my Cucci Cucci Couscous Muffins*

*Couscous is a partially refined product made from durum wheat, a variety of wheat most commonly used in making pasta. I like using couscous in tabouli because I find it lighter and more digestible than the more popular tabouli ingredient, bulghur. Similarly, I like using couscous in my muffins—I call them Cucci Cucci Couscous because they make me laugh!*

*P. S. You can now buy couscous in most larger commercial grocery stores. You should find it near the rice or in the specialty foods section.*

**Yield:** *12 muffins*

| Goodies | Dry Ingredients |
|---|---|
| 1/3 cup couscous | 2 cups whole-wheat pastry flour |
| 2 cloves minced garlic | 1/2 cup unbleached white flour |
| 1 cup boiling water | 1 tablespoon soy flour |
| 1/4 cup chopped scallions | 2 teaspoons baking powder |
| 4 tablespoons chopped fresh mint | 1 teaspoon baking soda |
| ( or 2 tablespoons dried mint) | 1/2 teaspoon sea salt |
| 6 tablespoons chopped fresh parsley | |
| (or 3 tablespoons dried parsley) | |

---

## Wet Ingredients

1 cup vegetable broth          1/4 cup olive oil

1/2 cup lemon juice            1 egg

---

1. Preheat oven to 400°.

2. Place the couscous and garlic in a medium saucepan. Add the boiling water and simmer for about 15 minutes while you prepare the remaining ingredients. (After the couscous absorbs the water, it should measure about 1 cup.)

3. Measure and sift the dry ingredients together in a large bowl. Sift a second time. Set aside.

4. Whisk the wet ingredients in a medium bowl or blend them in your food processor using the purée blade.

5. Add the couscous and the remaining goody ingredients (scallions, mint, and parsley) to the wet ingredients and toss to combine.

6. Pour the wet ingredients into the dry ingredients. Stir just until mixed. *Do not overstir.*

7. Spoon the batter into greased or papered baking tins. Fill each cup nearly to the top.

8. Bake for 15–20 minutes.

9. Cool in the baking tins for at least 10 minutes. Remove from the tins and brush the top of each muffin with olive oil.

**Serving suggestions:** Serve with Greek lemon soup and, of course, a Greek salad with lots of feta cheese. A side dish of sliced tomatoes goes beautifully.

# Falafel Muffins

*Falafel is a dish consisting of tasty little beanballs used in Middle Eastern pocket bread "sandwiches." I guess you could say that the sandwiches are the Middle East's version of a taco. Falafel is usually made by combining mashed chick peas (garbanzo beans), onions, garlic, bread crumbs, and herbs into a meatloaf-like mixture. Spoon-sized balls of the mixture are then rolled in flour or more bread crumbs and fried to a crispy finish. Falafel is stuffed in pocket bread with lettuce and tomato and covered with a special lemon-tahini sauce.*

*As you can imagine, falafel is one of those go-anywhere, eat-anytime treats because the ingredients can be prepared ahead of time and carried along on picnics or served later in the day. If you have never had this dish, I highly recommend that you give it a try. In the meantime, you can enjoy my Falafel Muffins.*

**Yield:** *14 muffins*

| Dry Ingredients | Wet Ingredients |
|---|---|
| 1 cup whole-wheat flour | 1 1/4 cups vegetable broth |
| 1 3/4 cups unbleached white flour | 1/2 cup lemon juice |
| 1/4 cup soy flour | 1/2 cup tahini |
| 1 tablespoon baking powder | 2 tablespoons soy sauce |
| 1 teaspoon baking soda | 1 egg (optional) * |

| Goodies | |
|---|---|
| 1 cup canned or home-cooked chick peas, well drained | 3 cloves minced garlic |
| 1/2 cup of liquid from the peas | 1 teaspoon ground cumin seed |
| 1 tablespoon chopped onion | 1 teaspoon ground coriander |
| 4 tablespoons chopped fresh parsley (or 3 tablespoons dried parsley) | 1/2 teaspoon chili powder |

1. Preheat oven to 400°.

2. Measure and sift the dry ingredients together in a large bowl. Sift a second time. Set aside.

3. Using the purée blade of your food processor, blend the wet ingredients. (If you do not have a food processor, a blender will work just as well.) Place the wet ingredients in a medium bowl.

4. Drain the chick peas, reserving 1/2 cup of liquid. Rinse the peas under cold water. Add the peas and the reserved liquid to the food processor and purée. (If you do not have a food processor, a blender will work just as well.) Add the peas to the wet ingredients.

5. Add the remaining goody ingredients (onion, parsley garlic, cumin, coriander, and chili powder) to the wet ingredients. Stir to a smooth consistency.

6. Pour the wet ingredients into the dry ingredients. Stir just until mixed. *Do not overstir.*

7. Spoon the batter into greased or papered baking tins. Fill each cup nearly to the top.

8. Bake for 15–20 minutes.

9. Cool in the baking tins for at least 10 minutes. Remove from the tins and brush the top of each muffin with olive oil.

**Serving suggestions:** Slice fresh tomato and cucumber on a bed of lettuce. Top with alfalfa sprouts and your favorite lemon/tahini dressing. Garnish with lots of fresh parsley. Serve steaming hot *Falafel Muffins*. These are also great for a picnic or with Middle Eastern cuisine such as tabouli or couscous salads.

---

\* The beans act as a binding agent so if you're restricting your egg consumption, you need not use an egg to hold these muffins together.

# French Onion Muffins

Most commercially prepared French onion soup is made with beef boullion. For years, I noticed that whenever French onion soup was on the menu, I would order it—no matter what else I ordered. But as I gradually reduced the red meat in my diet, I found I ordered French onion soup less and less frequently.

Several years ago, I discovered that the combination of toasted nutritional yeast flakes and soy sauce could be used to mimic the flavor of the usual beef boullion. It was a wonderful discovery and I liked the new flavor better than beef! So I've been enjoying French onion soup again—my own way.

"Why not a French onion muffin," I thought. "Surely it would satisfy in the same way." But a muffin from a soup recipe! Why not?

**Yield:** *12 muffins*

| Dry Ingredients | Goodies |
|---|---|
| 1 1/2 cups whole-wheat flour | 3 tablespoons chopped onion |
| 1 1/2 cups unbleached white flour | 2 cloves minced garlic |
| 1 tablespoon baking powder | 3/4 cup grated low-fat Swiss |
| 1/4 teaspoon ground pepper | or baby Swiss cheese |
| 1/2 cup nutritional yeast flakes | 1 1/2 tablespoons dried tarragon |

| Wet Ingredients | |
|---|---|
| 1 cup vegetable broth | 1 tablespoon soy sauce |
| 1 cup soy or cow's milk | 2 teaspoons dijon mustard |
| 1/4 cup olive oil | 2 teaspoons honey |
| 1 egg | |

1. Preheat oven to 400°.

2. Sift all the dry ingredients *except the nutritional yeast flakes* together in a large bowl. Sift a second time. Set aside.

3. In a small skillet, toast the nutritional yeast flakes until they begin to brown. Add the yeast to the dry ingredients and toss.

4. Whisk the wet ingredients in a medium bowl or blend them in your food processor using the purée blade.

5. Add the goodies to the wet ingredients. Stir to combine.

6. Pour the wet ingredients into the dry ingredients. Stir just until mixed. *Do not overstir.*

7. Spoon the batter into greased or papered baking tins. Fill each cup nearly to the top.

8. Bake for 15–20 minutes.

9. Cool in the baking tins for at least 10 minutes. Remove from the tins and brush the top of each muffin with olive oil.

**Serving suggestions:** Try these with sliced cheese, a Ceasar salad, and a bowl of vegetable consommé.

# Jewish Rye Muffins

*Somewhere in my distant past, I seem to recall seeing 10- to 12-foot loaves of Jewish rye bread displayed in a shop window. I watched the salesperson slice individual loaves from the mother loaf while salivating customers waited for their numbers to be called. The aroma of caraway and rye filled the room, and happy faces warmed the heart.*

*I wanted to warm hearts, too, so I created my Jewish Rye Muffins. Let me know if I have succeeded.*

**Yield:** *12 muffins*

| Goodies | Wet Ingredients |
|---|---|
| 1/2 cup rye flakes | 1 cup water |
| 1 1/2 tablespoons caraway seeds | 1/4 cup canola oil |
| 1 cup boiling water | 1 egg |
| | 2 tablespoons honey, warmed |

| Dry Ingredients | |
|---|---|
| 3/4 cup whole-wheat pastry flour | 2 teaspoons baking powder |
| 1/2 cup whole-wheat flour | 1/2 teaspoon baking soda |
| 1/2 cup unbleached white flour | 1 teaspoon sea salt |
| 1 1/2 cups rye flour | |

1. Preheat oven to 400°.

2. Using the purée blade of your food processor, grind the rye flakes until they resemble coarse meal. (If you do not have a food processor, a blender will work just as well.) Place both the rye meal and caraway seeds in a medium bowl and cover with the boiling water. Set aside.

3. Measure and sift the dry ingredients together in a large bowl. Sift a second time. Set aside.

4. Whisk the wet ingredients together in a small bowl or blend them in your food processor using the purée blade. Add the wet ingredients to the rye mixture and stir to combine.

5. Pour the wet ingredients into the dry ingredients. Stir just until mixed. *Do not overstir.*

6. Spoon the batter into greased or papered baking tins. Fill each cup nearly to the top.

7. Bake for 15–20 minutes.

8. Cool in the baking tins for at least 10 minutes. Remove from the tins and brush the top of each muffin with canola oil.

**Serving suggestions:** Try these with yellow or green split-pea soup to which you have added a bit of barley. Serve a nice tossed salad on the side.

# Mama Mia Muffins

As *Alice May Brock wrote in* Alice's Restaurant Cookbook, *"Tomatoes and oregano make it Italian; wine and tarragon make it French. Sour cream makes it Russian; lemon and cinnamon make it Greek. Soy makes it Chinese; garlic makes it good."*

*Garlic occupies a permanent place in my kitchen. You will notice that I use it everywhere. And why not? Italian caviar, as I've heard it called, makes everything I add it to taste great (except cherry cheesecake and pecan pie).*

*And garlic brings a miraculous healing quality to food. It is said that it relieves cold and asthma symptoms, aids digestion, soothes poison ivy, and pickles pimples.*

*Basically garlic bread in a muffin, my Mama Mia Muffins go with just about everything. Don't you think "Mama Mia Muffins" has a little ring to it?*

**Yield:** *12 muffins*

| Dry Ingredients | Goodies |
| --- | --- |
| 3 cups whole-wheat pastry flour | 5 cloves minced garlic |
| 1/2 cup unbleached white flour | 1 tablespoon dried basil |
| 1 tablespoon baking powder | 1 teaspoon dried oregano |
| 1/2 teaspoon sea salt | 3/4 cup grated parmesan cheese |
| 1/2 teaspoon paprika | |

| Wet Ingredients | Topping |
| --- | --- |
| 2 cups vegetable broth | sprinkling of paprika and |
| 1/2 cup olive oil | grated parmesan cheese |
| 1 egg | |

1. Preheat oven to 400°.

2. Measure and sift the dry ingredients together in a large bowl. Sift a second time. Set aside.

3. Whisk the wet ingredients in a medium bowl or blend them in your food processor using the purée blade.

4. Add the goodies to the wet ingredients and stir to combine.

5. Pour the wet ingredients into the dry ingredients. Stir just until mixed. *Do not overstir.*

6. Spoon the batter into greased or papered baking tins. Fill each cup nearly to the top.

7. Top each muffin with a sprinkling of paprika and grated parmesan cheese.

8. Bake for 15–20 minutes.

9. Cool in the baking tins for at least 10 minutes.

**Serving suggestions:** Enjoy these as you would garlic bread.

# Mexicali Corn Muffins

*One evening, I had dinner at a friend's. She served a spoon bread that had the guests licking their plates. Four of us ate two casseroles! I neglected to get the recipe from her, but I will never forget that combination of flavors. I re-created it for you in my Mexicali Corn Muffins. You may never eat plain old corn muffins again.*

*P. S. Make it easy on yourself. Buy the peppers and pimento already chopped and the cheese pre-grated.*

**Yield:** *12 muffins*

| Dry Ingredients | Goodies |
| --- | --- |
| 1/2 cup whole-wheat flour | 1 cup grated sharp cheddar cheese |
| 1 cup unbleached white flour | or Monterey jack cheese |
| 1 1/2 cups yellow cornmeal | 1 cup kernel corn |
| 1 tablespoon baking powder | 4-ounce can of chopped jalapeño |
| 1/2 teaspoon sea salt | peppers, well drained |
| | 4-ounce jar of chopped red |
| | pimento, well drained |

| Wet Ingredients | |
| --- | --- |
| 1 1/2 cups soy or cow's milk | 1 egg |
| 1/4 cup olive oil | 1 tablespoon honey |

1. Preheat oven to 400°.

2. Measure and sift the dry ingredients together in a large bowl. Sift a second time. Set aside.

3. Whisk the wet ingredients in a medium bowl or blend them in your food processor using the purée blade and place them in a medium bowl.

4. Add the goodies to the wet ingredients and stir to combine.

5. Pour the wet ingredients into the dry ingredients. Stir just until mixed. *Do not overstir.*

6. Spoon the batter into greased or papered baking tins. Fill each cup nearly to the top.

7. Bake for 15–20 minutes.

8. Cool in the baking tins for at least 10 minutes. Remove from the tins and brush the top of each muffin with olive oil.

**Serving suggestions:** These are a meal in themselves, but they go great with Mexican food, bean dishes, and/or a salad.

# Nickerpumpel Muffins

*You may not recognize these. They are Pumpernickel—spelled "crosswise." It's the way I used to say it when I was a kid—Nickerpumpel.*

*The darker the molasses and the darker the rye flour you use, the darker your Nickerpumpel Muffins will be. For a slightly richer dough, substitute 1 1/2 cups low-fat buttermilk and 1/2 cup water for the 2 cups soy or cow's milk.*

**Yield:** *12 muffins*

| Dry Ingredients | Wet Ingredients |
| --- | --- |
| 1 3/4 cups whole-wheat pastry flour | 2 cups soy or cow's milk |
| 1 cup dark rye flour | 1/4 cup canola oil |
| 1/2 cup buckwheat flour | 1 egg |
| 1/4 cup yellow cornmeal | 1/4 cup molasses, warmed |
| 1/4 cup soy flour | 1 teaspoon grated orange rind |
| 2 teaspoons baking powder | |
| 1 teaspoon baking soda | |
| 1 teaspoon sea salt | |
| 1 tablespoon caraway seeds | |

**Topping**

sprinkling of yellow cornmeal

1. Preheat oven to 400°.

2. Measure and sift all the dry ingredients *except the caraway seeds* together in a large bowl. Sift a second time. Add the caraway seeds and toss. Set aside.

3. Whisk the wet ingredients together in a small bowl or blend them in your food processor using the purée blade. Be sure the molasses is well blended.

4. Pour the wet ingredients into the dry ingredients. Stir just until mixed. *Do not overstir.*

5. Spoon the batter into greased or papered baking tins. Fill each cup nearly to the top.

6. Top each muffin with a sprinkling of cornmeal.

7. Bake for 15–20 minutes.

**Serving suggestions:** What can I say? These are great with a bowl of baked beans, or hot out of the oven with honey drizzled all over them.

# Pesto Muffins

What do you do when you can't decide between pasta with tomato sauce and pasta with pesto sauce? Tomato sauce is "real" Italian. I smell it, taste it, and instantly I'm beside Grandma and Aunt Clara as they stir a gigantic pot of sauce made from fresh garden tomatoes. But then there's my own melt-in-your-mouth creamy pesto sauce on linguini. And there's Grandma's tomato sauce. And there's creamy pesto sauce. And tomato. And pesto. And on and on. It's a dilemma, isn't it?

I realize that sometimes I have to have both. With my Pesto Muffins, I can enjoy pasta with tomato sauce and take my pesto on the side.

Make these with fresh basil if at all possible. There is no comparison to those made with dried herb. If you have your own favorite pesto recipe, substitute one cup of it for the goodies in this recipe.

*Yield: 12 muffins*

| Dry ingredients | Goodies |
| --- | --- |
| 2 1/2 cups whole-wheat pastry flour | 1/2 cup chopped fresh basil |
| 1/2 cup unbleached white flour | (or 1/4 cup dried basil) |
| 1/2 cup brown-rice flour | 2 cloves minced garlic |
| 2 teaspoons baking powder | 1/2 cup water |
| 1 teaspoon baking soda | 3/8 cup parmesan cheese |
| 1/2 teaspoon sea salt | 1/4 cup finely chopped pine nuts |
| | or sunflower seeds |

| Wet ingredients | |
| --- | --- |
| 1 cup vegetable broth | 1 egg |
| 1 cup soy or cow's milk | 2 teaspoons honey, warmed |
| 1/2 cup olive oil | |

1. Preheat oven to 400°.

2. Measure and sift the dry ingredients together in a large bowl. Sift a second time. Set aside.

3. Whisk the wet ingredients together in a medium bowl or blend them in your food processor using the purée blade.

4. Add the goodies to the wet ingredients and stir to combine.

5. Pour the wet ingredients into the dry ingredients. Stir just until mixed. *Do not overstir.*

6. Spoon the batter into greased or papered baking tins. Fill each cup nearly to the top.

7. Bake for 15–20 minutes.

8. Cool in the baking tins for at least 10 minutes. Remove from the tins and brush the top of each muffin with olive oil.


**Serving suggestions:** If you have never tried muffins with Italian dishes, do it now. These are truly outrageous!

# Polka Dottie Muffins

*When I eat sweet peas, I feel as if I am getting a blood transfusion—the feeling I imagine my car gets when the oil is changed. Sweet peas have a heartiness that sends a healing warmth throughout my body.*

*I just had to include a muffin with sweet peas the way I like to eat them— with a touch of soysage, sage, and tomato. When baked, these muffins look like green and red "polka dotties."*

**Yield:** *10 muffins*

| Goodies | Dry Ingredients |
| --- | --- |
| 1/4 pound hot spicy *soysage* (about 1 1/4 cups) | 2 cups whole-wheat pastry flour 1/4 cup unbleached white flour |
| 1 tablespoon canola oil | 1/4 cup millet flour |
| 8-ounce can of sweet peas, (about 1 cup drained) | 1 tablespoon baking powder 1/4 teaspoon salt |
| 2 teaspoons rubbed sage | |
| 1 teaspoon dried thyme | |

| Wet Ingredients | |
| --- | --- |
| 1 cup tomato juice | |
| 1 cup vegetable broth | |
| 1/4 cup canola oil | |
| 1 egg | |

1. Using a medium skillet, crumble and sauté the soysage in 1 tablespoon canola oil until lightly browned. Remove the soysage from the skillet and drain well on a paper towel to remove the excess oil. If necessary, crumble large chunks of soysage. Set aside.

2. Preheat oven to 400°.

3. Measure and sift the dry ingredients together in a large bowl. Sift a second time. Set aside.

4. Whisk the wet ingredients in a medium bowl or blend them in your food processor using the purée blade.

5. Drain the sweet peas, rinse and drain again. Add the soysage, sweet peas and remaining goody ingredients (sage and thyme) to the wet ingredients. Stir to combine.

6. Pour the wet ingredients into the dry ingredients. Stir just until mixed. *Do not overstir.*

7. Spoon the batter into greased or papered baking tins. Fill each cup nearly to the top.

8. Bake for 15–20 minutes.

9. Cool in the baking tins for at least 10 minutes. Remove from the tins and brush the top of each muffin with canola oil.

**Serving suggestions:** Wash these down with a chilled vegetable juice chaser.

# Pomme-de-Terre-With-Spinach Muffins

*The only word I remember from my seventh-grade French class is "pomme de terre," the French word for potato. Pomme de terre. Pomme de terre. I used to love to say it. But even more than saying it, I loved to eat it—especially in piping hot potato soup.*

*Recently, I gave my standard potato soup recipe a boost. My friend Michele, who has made several trips to Paris this year, told me about a potato soup she enjoyed there. What made it special, she said, was the addition of spinach and a hint of mace. I took her word for it and added these to my soup—and to my potato muffins. Voila! Le-Pomme-de Terre-With-Spinach Muffins.*

**Yield:** *12 muffins*

| Dry Ingredients | Wet Ingredients |
|---|---|
| 1 3/4 cups whole-wheat pastry flour | 1 cup vegetable broth |
| 1/2 cup unbleached white flour | 1 1/2 cups soy or cow's milk |
| 2 teaspoons baking powder | 1/4 cup olive oil |
| 1/2 teaspoon baking soda | 1 egg |
| 1/4 teaspoon black pepper | |
| 1 1/2 teaspoons sea salt | |
| 1/4 teaspoon ground mace | |

| Goodies | |
|---|---|
| 2 tablespoons chopped scallions (about 2) | 1 cup instant potato flakes |
| 1 clove minced garlic | (not powdered potatoes) |
| 1/2 cup firmly packed chopped spinach (fresh or frozen) | |

1. Preheat oven to 400°.

2. Measure and sift the dry ingredients together in a large bowl. Sift a second time. Set aside.

3. Whisk the wet ingredients in a medium bowl or blend them in your food processor using the purée blade.

4. Add the goodies to the wet ingredients and stir to combine. (Frozen chopped spinach must be defrosted and drained before using; squeeze out excess water.)

5. Pour the wet ingredients into the dry ingredients. Stir just until mixed. *Do not overstir.*

6. Spoon the batter into greased or papered baking tins. Fill each cup nearly to the top.

7. Bake for 15–20 minutes.

8. Cool in the baking tins for at least 10 minutes. Remove from the tins and brush the top of each muffin with olive oil.

**Serving suggestions:** Serve adorable little mini-muffins (this recipe makes about 36) in baskets. Bake the mini-muffins for 10–15 minutes.

# Sea-Veggie Surprise Muffins

My earliest memories of seaweed are of slimy green or stringy brown stuff floating in the ocean. It attracted jelly fish and stinging insects, which meant we couldn't go in the water. Yuk! The idea that somebody might eat the stuff never entered my mind!

More recently, my friend John from California encouraged me to try his favorite seaweed dish made with hijiki and carrots.What can I say? It was wonderful. Really! I couldn't believe how delicious it tasted. Now, I am enjoying hijiki again in my Sea-Veggie Surprise Muffins. The brown spaghetti-like tendrils of hijiki coupled with the orange strands of shredded carrot appear as veins throughout the muffins—very attractive. And the sea-veggie flavor is a great accompaniment to most vegetarian meals.

**Yield:** *12 muffins*

| Goodies | Wet Ingredients |
|---|---|
| 1/2 cup dried hijiki | 2 cups vegetable broth |
| 1 cup grated carrot | 1/4 cup canola oil |
| 2 cloves minced garlic | 2 teaspoons toasted sesame oil |
| | 1 egg |
| | 2 tablespoons soy sauce |

| Dry Ingredients | |
|---|---|
| 1 cup whole-wheat flour | 2 teaspoons baking powder |
| 1 3/4 cups unbleached white flour | 1 teaspoon baking soda |
| 2 tablespoons soy flour | |

1. Cover the hijiki with warm water and soak for 20 minutes. Drain the hijiki, rinse well with cold water, drain again, and place it in a medium bowl. If the strands are particularly long, break or chop them into 1-inch lengths.

2. Add the carrot and the garlic to the hijiki and toss to combine.

3. Preheat oven to 400°.

4. Measure and sift the dry ingredients together in a large bowl. Sift a second time. Set aside.

5. Whisk the wet ingredients in a small bowl or blend them in your food processor using the purée blade. Add the wet ingredients to the goodies. Stir to combine.

6. Pour the wet ingredients into the dry ingredients. Stir just until mixed. *Do not overstir.*

7. Spoon the batter into greased or papered baking tins. Fill each cup nearly to the top.

8. Bake for 15–20 minutes.

9. Cool in the baking tins for at least 10 minutes. Remove from the tins and brush the top of each muffin with canola oil.

**Serving suggestions:** Try these with a bowl of miso broth and a salad, stir-fried veggies with tofu, or any Japanese cuisine.

# Seedy Muffins

There are bagels and there are bagels. To me, a "real" bagel is one that starts with a firm foundation of wholesome dough and ends with a sprinkling of one kind of seed or another. When it comes to bagels, only seedy ones will do.

To my way of thinking, the ultimate bagel is alive and flourishing in a bagel shop that my friend Barbara and I like to frequent. This is called the "Everything Bagel" because it includes everything that one could possible want in a "real" bagel—poppy seeds, sesame seeds, and carraway seeds—with a touch of garlic. My Seedy Muffins are a spin-off of the "Everything Bagel." They are a tribute to good eating and to breakfast with Barbara!

**Yield:** 12 muffins

| Dry Ingredients | Wet Ingredients |
| --- | --- |
| 1 1/2 cups whole-wheat pastry flour | 1 1/2 cups soy or cow's milk |
| 1 cup unbleached white flour | 1/2 cup tahini |
| 1/2 cup rye flour | 1/4 cup canola oil |
| 1 tablespoon soy flour | 1 egg |
| 2 teaspoons baking powder | 2 tablespoons honey, warmed |
| 1 teaspoon baking soda | |
| 1/4 teaspoon black pepper | |

| Goodies | |
| --- | --- |
| 2 tablespoons caraway seed | 1 teaspoon sea salt |
| 1 tablespoon hulled sesame seeds | 2 tablespoons canola oil |
| 4 tablespoons roasted sunflower seeds | 4 cloves minced garlic |
| 1 tablespoon poppy seeds | |

1. Preheat oven to 400°.

2. Measure and sift the dry ingredients together in a large bowl. Sift a second time.

3. Using the purée blade of your food processor, grind the carraway, sesame, sunflower and poppy seeds by pulsing the processor blade a few times. Add the remaining goody ingredients (oil and garlic) and pulse the processor blade a few more times. (If you do not have a food processor, grind the seeds using a hand-operated grinder and add the oil and garlic.) Retain 4 tablespoons of the mixture to sprinkle on top of each muffin (see step 7). Add the remaining seed mixture to the dry ingredients. Toss to combine. Set aside.

4. Using the purée blade of your food processor, blend the wet ingredients. (If you do not have a food processor, a blender will work just as well.)

5. Pour the wet ingredients into the dry ingredients. Stir just until mixed. *Do not overstir.*

6. Spoon the batter into greased or papered baking tins. Fill each cup nearly to the top.

7. Top each muffin with approximately 1 teaspoon of the seed mixture.

8. Bake for 15–20 minutes.

9. Cool in the baking tins for at least 10 minutes.

*Serving suggestions:* Plenty seedy—i.e., full of seeds—these muffins are a great go-along with just about any meal.

# Soysage Pizza Muffins

Some of my happiest early childhood memories are of sitting in grandma's kitchen while she simmered tomato sauce for pasta and pizza. She always included a substantial portion of sausage that she and grandpa had made using lots of garlic and fennel. The aroma was outrageous . . . and the flavor . . . ! The garlic made it Italian and the fennel seed made it grandma's.

My diet has changed and I've switched to soysage instead of sausage in my tomato sauce, but I still add plenty of the fennel flavor that was so attractive to me as a child. As in grandma's sauce, fennel makes my Soysage Pizza Muffins one-of-a-kind.

**Yield:** 14 muffins

| Goodies | Dry Ingredients |
| --- | --- |
| 1/2 cup sun-dried tomatoes | 2 cups whole-wheat pastry flour |
| 3/4 cup boiling water | 1 1/2 cups whole-wheat flour |
| 1/4 pound hot, spicy soysage | 1/2 cup unbleached white flour |
| (about 1 1/4 cups) | 2 teaspoons baking powder |
| 1 tablespoon olive oil | 1 teaspoon baking soda |
| 1 1/2 cups grated mozarella cheese | 1/2 teaspoon sea salt |
| 1 clove minced garlic | |
| 1 tablespoon fennel seed | |
| 1/2 teaspoon dried oregano | |

| Wet Ingredients | |
| --- | --- |
| 1 cup tomato juice | 1 egg |
| 1 cup soy or cow's milk | 2 teaspoons honey |
| 1/4 cup olive oil | |

1. Chop the sun-dried tomatoes into pea-sized bits. Place them in a medium bowl and cover them with the boiling water. Set aside to soak for about 20 minutes.

2. Preheat oven to 400°.

3. Using a medium skillet, crumble and sauté the soysage in 1 tablespoon olive oil until lightly browned. Remove the soysage from the skillet and drain well on a paper towel to remove the excess oil. Add the soysage and 3/4 cup of the mozarella cheese to the soaking tomatoes. Retain the remaining 3/4 cup to top each muffin (see Step 8). Add the remaining goody ingredients (garlic, fennel seed, and oregano). Stir to combine.

4. Measure and sift the dry ingredients together in a large bowl. Sift a second time. Set aside.

5. Whisk the wet ingredients in a small bowl or blend them in your food processor using the purée blade. Add the wet ingredients to the goodies and stir to combine.

6. Pour the wet ingredients into the dry ingredients. Stir just until mixed. *Do not overstir.*

7. Spoon the batter into greased or papered baking tins. Fill each cup nearly to the top.

8. Top each muffin with a scant tablespoon of grated mozarella cheese before baking.

9. Bake for 15–20 minutes.

10. Cool in the baking tins for at least 10 minutes.


**Serving suggestions:** I think you will agree that these are a meal in themselves. At most, they could do with a salad on the side.

# Spanakopita Muffins

*Perhaps more than any other ethnic group, the Greeks have known and enjoyed the wonders of spinach. Spanakopita is a spinach pie, of sorts, enhanced with feta cheese and nutmeg. A current-day take-off on spanokopita can be found in spinach-stuffed croissants and little spinach pies. These, too, are very delicious. Just thinking about spinach pies makes my mouth water. I had to give Spanakopita Muffins a try. And am I glad I did!*

**Yield:** *12 muffins*

| Dry Ingredients | Wet Ingredients |
| --- | --- |
| 1 1/2 cups whole-wheat flour | 1 1/2 cups vegetable broth |
| 1 1/2 cups unbleached white flour | 1/4 cup olive oil |
| 1 tablespoon baking powder | 1 egg |

| Goodies | |
| --- | --- |
| 1/2 cup low-fat cottage cheese | 2 cloves minced garlic |
| 1 cup crumbled feta cheese | 1 tablespoon honey, warmed |
| 1/2 cup firmly packed chopped spinach (fresh or frozen) | 1/4 teaspoon ground mace |

1. Preheat oven to 400°.

2. Measure and sift the dry ingredients together in a large bowl. Sift a second time. Set aside.

3. Whisk the wet ingredients together in a medium bowl or blend in your food processor using the purée blade.

4. Add the goodies to the wet ingredients and stir to combine. (Frozen spinach must be defrosted and drained before using; squeeze out extra water.) *Do not use a blender or food processor.*

5. Pour the wet ingredients into the dry ingredients. Stir just until mixed. *Do not overstir.*

6. Spoon the batter into greased or papered baking tins. Fill each cup nearly to the top.

7. Bake for 15–20 minutes.

8. Cool in the baking tins for at least 10 minutes. Remove from the tins and brush the top of each muffin with olive oil.

*Serving suggestions:* Serve with a Greek salad, of course!

# Spinach-Lentil Muffins

One meal that never ceases to dazzle company is my lentil-spinach loaf. Well it's not really my lentil-spinach loaf. My friend Annie gave me her recipe years ago, and I have made it my old stand-by ever since. I think people like how the loaf's broad range of flavors seems to contact every tastebud in the mouth.

Spinach-Lentil Muffins are no less dazzling. I usually make these with chopped frozen spinach. All I have to do is thaw the package, squeeze out the excess moisture, and I am ready to go.

P. S. Several of my muffins call for chopped spinach. Why not plan ahead? Make my Spanakopita Muffins (see page 138), Sun-Dried Tomato Muffins (see page 144), or Pomme-de-Terre-With-Spinach Muffins (see page 130) at the same time and freeze them for later use.

Yield: 12 muffins

| Dry Ingredients | Wet Ingredients |
|---|---|
| 1/2 cup whole-wheat pastry flour | 1 cup vegetable broth |
| 1 cup whole-wheat flour | 1/2 cup soy or cow's milk |
| 1/2 cup unbleached white flour | 1/4 cup olive oil |
| 1/4 cup millet flour | 1 egg |
| 1 tablespoon baking powder | 1 1/2 tablespoons soy sauce |
| 1/2 teaspoon baking soda | |
| 1/2 teaspoon sea salt | |
| 1/2 teaspoon black pepper | |
| 1/8 to 1/4 teaspoon cayenne | |
| (depending on your taste) | |

## Goodies

| | |
|---|---|
| 1/2 cup canned or home-cooked lentils | 1 tablespoon ground cumin |
| 1/2 cup firmly packed chopped spinach (fresh or frozen) | 1 teaspoon ground cardamom |
| 1 tablespoon chopped onion | 1 1/2 cups grated extra sharp cheddar cheese |

1. Preheat oven to 400°.

2. Measure and sift the dry ingredients together in a large bowl. Sift a second time. Set aside.

3. Whisk the wet ingredients in a medium bowl or blend them in your food processor using the purée blade and pour them into a medium bowl.

4. Add the goodies to the wet ingredients and stir to combine. (Frozen spinach must be defrosted and drained before using; squeeze out excess water.)

5. Pour the wet ingredients into the dry ingredients. Stir just until mixed. *Do not overstir.*

6. Spoon the batter into greased or papered baking tins. Fill each cup nearly to the top.

7. Bake for 20–25 minutes.

8. Cool in the baking tins for at least 10 minutes. Remove from the tins and brush the top of each muffin with olive oil.

**Serving suggestions:** Slice *Spinach-Lentil Muffins* into four slices and spread each with hot salsa. Serve with a garden fresh salad and ranch dressing.

# Spring Roll Muffins

*What we call "egg roll" in this country is called "spring roll" in China because it is served during the spring festivals. I like mine fried crispy but not greasy and smothered in apricot duck sauce. But what I really like is the combination of flavors in each bite. "Why not bring this same combination to a muffin?" I thought. That way I won't have to wait until I go to Chinese restaurants to enjoy the tastes I love. Sound crazy? Confucius says, "Try these before you turn up your nose. Mmm. Mmm. Mmm!"*

**Yield:** *12 muffins*

| Dry Ingredients | Wet Ingredients |
| --- | --- |
| 2 cups whole-wheat pastry flour | 1 1/2 cups vegetable broth |
| 1/2 cup brown-rice flour | 1/4 cup canola oil |
| 1 tablespoon baking powder | 4 teaspoons toasted sesame oil |
| | 1 egg |
| | 1 tablespoon rice syrup, warmed |
| | (or 1 teaspoon honey, warmed) |
| | 1 tablespoon soy sauce |

| Goodies | |
| --- | --- |
| 1 clove minced garlic | 2 tablespoons chopped scallions |
| 1 tablespoon grated ginger root | (about 2 whole) |
| (or 1 1/2 teaspoons powdered | 15 chopped water chestnuts |
| ginger) | 15 chopped dried apricots |
| 6 tablespoons chopped celery | |

1. Preheat oven to 400°.

2. Measure and sift the dry ingredients together in a large bowl. Sift a second time. Set aside.

3. Whisk the wet ingredients in a small bowl or blend them in your food processor using the purée blade.

4. Add the goodies to the wet ingredients and stir to combine.

5. Pour the wet ingredients into the dry ingredients. Stir just until mixed. *Do not overstir.*

6. Spoon the batter into greased or papered baking tins. Fill each cup nearly to the top.

7. Bake for 15–20 minutes.

8. Cool in the baking tins for at least 10 minutes. Remove from the tins and brush the top of each muffin with canola oil.

**Serving suggestions:** With one from column A and two from column B.

# Steven's Sun-Dried-Tomato Muffins

*My friend Steven is an excellent cook. He has a knack for making even the simplest dishes look and taste elegant. He uses seasonings in artistic, clever, and creative ways. Once, years ago, he served a pizza that had a deep, deep tomato flavor. Even my discriminating taste buds could not identify the ingredient that resulted in such richness. Shortly thereafter, I noticed the same flavor on Steven's crab salad. I suspected the red mushy chunks that looked like pimento, but didn't taste like pimento. "What are these little red things?" I asked. "They are so delicious."*

*"Gloria, you must try to stay abreast of the current fashions," he quipped. "Those little red things are sun-dried tomatoes, and they are the latest thing in palate-pleasers."*

*Since then, I have learned that it takes as many as 18 pounds of fresh tomatoes to make 1 pound of sun-dried tomatoes. No wonder they are so rich!*

*Anyway, thank you, Steven. You are the inspiration for my Sun-Dried-Tomato Muffins.*

**Yield:** *14 muffins*

## Goodies

| | |
|---|---|
| 1/2 cup sun-dried tomatoes | 3/4 cup grated parmesan cheese |
| 3/4 cup hot water | 1/2 cup firmly packed |
| 3/4 cup whole pine nuts or |    chopped spinach (fresh or frozen) |
|    chopped walnuts | 1 tablespoon dried oregano |
| 2 cloves minced garlic | 1 tablespoon dried basil |

| Dry Ingredients | Wet ingredients |
|---|---|
| 1 1/2 cups whole-wheat flour | 2 cups tomato juice |
| 1 1/2 cups unbleached white flour | 1/4 cup olive oil |
| 2 teaspoons baking powder | 1 egg |
| 1 teaspoon baking soda | 1 tablespoon honey |
| 1/4 teaspoon black pepper | |

1. Chop the sun-dried tomatoes into pea-sized bits. Place them in a medium bowl and cover them with the boiling water. Set aside to soak for about 20 minutes.

2. Preheat oven to 400°.

3. Measure and sift the dry ingredients together in a large bowl. Sift a second time. Set aside.

4. Add the nuts and the remaining goody ingredients (garlic, cheese, spinach, oregano, and basil) to the soaking tomatoes. Stir to combine.

5. Whisk the wet ingredients in a small bowl or blend them in your food processor using the purée blade. Add the wet ingredients to the goodies and stir to combine.

6. Pour the wet ingredients into the dry ingredients. Stir just until mixed. *Do not overstir.*

7. Spoon the batter into greased or papered baking tins. Fill each cup nearly to the top.

8. Bake for 15–20 minutes.

9. Cool in the baking tins for at least 10 minutes. Remove from the tins and brush the top of each muffin with olive oil.

**Serving suggestions:** If you serve these with pasta, make it a rather passive and unassuming pasta dish. *Sun-Dried-Tomato Muffins* need no help in bringing you pleasure.

# Wild Rice Stuffin' Muffins

*I've always thought of wild rice as an exotic import from a far away land. But most of the wild rice consumed in this country comes from the Great Lakes!*

*I especially enjoy wild rice as a stuffing. Wild rice stuffin' can be a nice change from the bread crumb varieties, and it goes very well with sweet, fruity ingredients like oranges, raisins, walnuts, and dried apples. I usually serve it with a buttery orange sauce. So when I made my Wild Rice Stuffin' Muffins, I included the same mouth-watering combination of ingredients and topped each muffin with an orange glaze.*

*P. S. I prefer the flavor of golden raisins with wild rice, but you can use dark raisins if you like. (For more on golden versus dark raisins, turn to page 102.)*

**Yield:** *12 muffins*

| Goodies | Wet Ingredients |
|---|---|
| 2/3 cup wild rice | 1 cup vegetable broth |
| 1 1/2 cups water | 1/2 cup orange juice concentrate |
| 1/2 cup chopped dried apples | 1/4 cup canola oil |
| 1/2 cup chopped walnuts | 1 egg |
| 1/2 cup golden raisins | 1/4 cup all-fruit orange marmalade |
| 1/2 teaspoon ground thyme | |
| 1/2 teaspoon rubbed sage | |
| 1/8 teaspoon ground nutmeg | |

### Dry Ingredients

| | |
|---|---|
| 1 1/2 cups whole-wheat pastry flour | 2 teaspoons baking powder |
| 1/2 cup whole-wheat flour | 1 teaspoon baking soda |
| 1/4 cup brown-rice flour | 1/2 teaspoon sea salt |

## Topping

Orange Glaze (see *Gloria's Glorious Glazes* on page 168)

1. Rinse the rice in cold water. Drain well. Repeat. Boil the 1 1/2 cups of water and add the rice. Reduce heat to low, cover, and continue to cook for about 45 minutes. (This makes 2 cups of cooked wild rice.) Remove rice from heat, cool, and set aside.

2. Preheat oven to 400°.

3. Measure and sift the dry ingredients together in a large bowl. Sift a second time. Set aside.

4. Whisk the wet ingredients in a medium bowl or blend them in your food processor using the purée blade.

5. Add the wild rice and the remaining goody ingredients (dried apples, walnuts, raisins, thyme, sage, and nutmeg) to the wet ingredients. Stir to combine.

6. Pour the wet ingredients into the dry ingredients. Stir just until mixed. *Do not overstir.*

7. Spoon the batter into greased or papered baking tins. Fill each cup nearly to the top.

8. Bake for 15–20 minutes.

9. While the muffins bake, prepare the Orange Glaze.

10. When the muffins are done, cool them for about 15 minutes in the baking tins. Remove from the tins and coat each muffin with enough glaze to cover the top surface. Cool for an additional 10 minutes before you dig in.

**Serving suggestions:** If you are a poultry eater, try these with cornish game hens or duck.

# DESSERT MUFFINS

*For those who like this sort of thing,*
*this is the sort of thing they like.*

Max Bierbohm

I've never met a dessert I didn't like. On occasion, I've met people who didn't like desserts, but I didn't like these people. I got the feeling that when it came to having a good time, they would only go so far. I guess I like being playful better than being grown-up.

Let's face it, desserts bring out the kid in nearly all of us. Rare is the person who doesn't giggle and grin when the waitperson clears the plates and asks, "Care for any dessert?"

"Oh, I shouldn't. I couldn't. What do you have?"

If you have ever felt any reservation or guilt when giving an affirmative reply to the call for dessert, your world has just changed dramatically. This chapter of *Gloria's Glorious Muffins* offers a wonderful collection of muffins with enough sweetness to satisfy even the most stubborn sweet tooth and enough wholesome goodness to kiss the guilties goodbye. Unlike cupcakes that are made with lots of sugar and eggs, muffins are a wholesome dessert. Moms can breathe easy when kids want desserts, and weight-watchers can smile all the way to the scales.

# Almond Cookie Muffins

*What I had in mind with these muffins is a re-creation of the flavors in those wonderful Amaretto cookies that I enjoy in Italian restaurants and specialty food stores. You know, the crunchy ones with assorted color wrappers. Their rich, sweet almond flavor is yummy.*

*My Almond Cookie Muffins with a drizzle of Chocolate Fudge Sauce are an impressive finale for any cuisine, but you will find them a particularly mouth-watering topper for your favorite Italian meal.*

*Remember, any muffin with nuts is not particularly low in fat. These would not be your best choice if fat is an issue in your diet.*

**Yield:** *12 muffins*

| Dry Ingredients | Goodies |
| --- | --- |
| 1 3/4 cups whole-wheat flour | 1 1/2 cups coarsely chopped |
| 1 cup unbleached white flour | roasted almonds |
| 3/4 cup brown-rice flour | |
| 2 teaspoons baking powder | |
| 1 teaspoon baking soda | |
| 1/2 teaspoon sea salt | |
| 1/2 teaspoon ground cardamom | |

**Wet Ingredients**

1 cup apple juice concentrate
1 cup soy or cow's milk
1/4 cup canola oil
1 egg
1 teaspoon almond extract

1. Preheat oven to 400°.

2. Measure and sift the dry ingredients together in a large bowl. Sift a second time. Set aside.

3. Add 1 1/8 cups of the chopped almonds to the dry ingredients and toss. Retain the remaining 3/8 cup of almonds to top each muffin (see Step 7).

4. Whisk the wet ingredients in a small bowl or blend them in your food processor using the purée blade.

5. Pour the wet ingredients into the dry ingredients. Stir just until mixed. *Do not overstir.*

6. Spoon the batter into greased or papered baking tins. Fill each cup nearly to the top.

7. Top each muffin with approximately 1 1/2 teaspoons chopped almonds.

8. Bake for 15–20 minutes.

9. Cool in the baking tins for at least 10 minutes.

**Serving suggestions:** Slice *Almond Cookie Muffins* into four slices and fan the slices on your favorite dessert plate. Drizzle *Chocolate Fudge Sauce* (see *Gloria's Glorious Muffin Sauces* on page 154) over the slices and garnish with fresh cherries.

# *Gloria's Glorious Muffin Sauces*

## Vanilla Custard Sauce

**Yield:** *2 cups*

2 tablespoons shortening
(canola oil, melted soy
margarine, or melted butter)
2 tablespoons cornstarch
2 cups soy or cow's milk

3 tablespoons honey
1 tablespoon Sucanat or
brown sugar
2 teaspoons vanilla
extract
1 teaspoon lemon juice
dash ground nutmeg

1. Using the purée blade of your food processor (or your blender), blend the shortening, cornstarch, milk, honey, and Sucanat or brown sugar. Make sure that the cornstarch lumps are dissolved.

2. Pour the mixture into a medium saucepan. Stirring frequently, cook the mixture over low heat until it thickens. Remove from heat.

3. Add the vanilla, lemon juice, and nutmeg. Stir to a smooth consistency.

4. Serve warm.

# Chocolate-Raspberry Custard Sauce

*Yield: 2 cups*

2 tablespoons shortening
(canola oil, melted soy
margarine, or melted butter)
2 tablespoons cornstarch
2 cups soy or cow's milk

1/4 cup cocoa
3 tablespoons Sucanat or
brown sugar
1/4 cup all-fruit
raspberry jam
1 teaspoon vanilla
extract

1. Using the purée blade of your food processor (or your blender), blend the shortening, cornstarch, milk, cocoa, Sucanat or brown sugar, and jam. Make sure that the cornstarch lumps are dissolved.

2. Pour the mixture into a medium saucepan. Stirring frequently, cook the mixture over low heat until it thickens. Remove from heat.

3. Add the vanilla. Stir to a smooth consistency.

4. Serve warm.

# Chocolate Fudge Sauce

*Yield: 1 cup*

4 tablespoons shortening
(canola oil, soy margarine,
or butter)
1/2 cup cocoa

1 cup water
1 cup Sucanat or
    brown sugar
1 teaspoon vanilla
extract

1. Melt the shortening in a medium saucepan.

2. Stir in the cocoa until it dissolves.

3. Gradually stir in the water using a wire whisk.

4. Add the Sucanat or brown sugar. Cook over low heat for 30 minutes.

5. Remove from heat. Add the vanilla extract. Stir.

6. Serve warm. (The sauce will thicken as it cools.)

# Carob Sauce

*Yield: 1 cup*

| | |
|---|---|
| 1/2 cup carob powder | 1/4 cup Sucanat or |
| 3 tablespoons shortening | brown sugar |
| (canola oil, soy | 1/4 cup honey |
| margarine, or butter) | 2 teaspoons vanilla |
| 1/2 cup water | extract |

1. Toast the carob powder in a medium skillet until it begins to smell toasty.

2. Add the canola oil, soy margarine, or butter and stir until the carob is coated.

3. Gradually stir in the water using a wire whisk.

4. Add the Sucanat or brown sugar and the honey. Cook over low heat for 30 minutes.

5. Remove from heat. Add the vanilla extract. Stir.

6. Serve warm. (The sauce will thicken as it cools.)

# Boston Brown Muffins

*The buttermilk in my Boston Brown Muffins makes them especially moist—not unlike the steamed bread that inspired them. These are great muffins for breakfast and for the holidays, but I put them in the dessert section because they are sweet and satisfying enough to top any meal.*

**Yield:** *12 muffins*

| Dry Ingredients | Wet Ingredients |
| --- | --- |
| 1 1/4 cups whole-wheat pastry flour | 1/2 cup apple juice concentrate |
| 1/2 cup unbleached white flour | 1 1/2 cups buttermilk |
| 1/4 cup yellow cornmeal | 1/4 cup canola oil |
| 1/2 cup rye flour | 1 egg |
| 1/2 cup buckwheat flour | |
| 2 teaspoons baking powder | |
| 1 teaspoon baking soda | |
| 1/2 cup Sucanat or brown sugar | |
| 1/2 teaspoon sea salt | |

| Goodies | Topping (optional) |
| --- | --- |
| 1 1/2 cups raisins | *Sucanat or Brown Sugar Glaze* |
| 1 cup roasted sunflower seeds | (see *Gloria's Glorious Glazes* |
| | on page 169.) |

1. Preheat oven to 400°.

2. Measure and sift the dry ingredients together in a large bowl. Sift a second time. Set aside.

3. Whisk the wet ingredients in a small bowl or blend them in your food processor using the purée blade.

4. Add the goodies to the wet ingredients and stir to distribute them evenly throughout.

5. Pour the wet ingredients into the dry ingredients. Stir just until mixed. *Do not overstir.*

6. Spoon the batter into greased or papered baking tins. Fill each cup nearly to the top.

7. Bake for 15–20 minutes.

8. Optional: While the muffins bake, prepare the *Sucanat or Brown Sugar Glaze*.

9. When the muffins are done, cool them for about 15 minutes in the baking tins. Remove from the tins and coat each muffin with enough glaze to cover the top surface. Cool an additional 10 minutes before you dig in.

**Serving suggstions:** Just slice and enjoy them! Or, if you do not make the topping, try these with *Maple Butter Spread* (see *Gloria's Glorious Muffin Butters and Spreads* on page 56).

# Carrot Conglomeration Muffins

*Sometimes you just want to put everything but the kitchen sink in your muffins. Why not? Especially when "everything" includes carrot, coconut, and apples. And if you have ever had carrot cake with dried pineapple instead of raisins, you know why I have offered that as an option. If not, try it!*

*Kids love it when I make these into mini-muffins so they can just pop them in their mouths. Carrot Conglomeration Muffins usually turn out to be everybody's favorite!*

**Yield:** *12 muffins or 36 mini-muffins*

| Dry Ingredients | Wet Ingredients |
| --- | --- |
| 1/2 cup whole-wheat pastry flour | 3/4 cup apple juice concentrate |
| 1/2 cup whole-wheat flour | 1/4 cup soy or cow's milk |
| 1 cup unbleached white flour | 1/4 cup canola oil |
| 2 teaspoons baking powder | 1 egg |
| 1 teaspoon baking soda | 2 teaspoons vanilla extract |
| 1/2 teaspoon sea salt | 2 tablespoons orange rind |
| 1/4 cup Sucanat or brown sugar | |
| 2 teaspoons ground cinnamon | |

### Goodies

1 cup chopped apples (*Do not grate.*)
1 cup grated carrots
3/4 cup raisins (or dried pineapple)
1/2 cup coconut
3/4 cup roasted sunflower seeds

1. Preheat oven to 400°.

2. Measure and sift the dry ingredients together in a large bowl. Sift a second time. Set aside.

3. Whisk the wet ingredients in a medium bowl or blend them in your food processor using the purée blade.

4. Add the goodies to the wet ingredients and stir to combine.

5. Pour the wet ingredients into the dry ingredients. Stir just until mixed. *Do not overstir.*

6. Spoon the batter into greased or papered baking tins. Fill each cup nearly to the top.

7. Bake for 15–20 minutes for regular muffins or 10–15 minutes for mini-muffins.

8. Cool in the baking tins for at least 10 minutes. Remove from the tins and brush the top of each muffin with canola oil.

**Serving suggestions:** Here's another muffin that is great with *Apple Butter Spread* (see *Gloria's Glorious Muffin Butters and Spreads* on page 56).

# Cinnamon Sticky Muffins

*While in high school, I worked at MaryAnn Donuts in Allentown, Pennsylvania. Mr. Wons and Harry, master bakers to my way of thinking, made the best sticky buns I have ever tasted. They were moist, and cakey, and covered with nuts. Hot out of the oven, they were impossible to resist.*

*My Cinnamon Sticky Muffins draw the same response. Try making these with jumbo muffin tins instead of the usual 3-inch ones.*

**Yield:** *18 muffins or 9 jumbo muffins*

| Dry Ingredients | Wet Ingredients |
|---|---|
| 1 1/2 cups whole-wheat pastry flour | 1 1/2 cups applesauce |
| 1/2 cup whole-wheat flour | 1 cup soy or cow's milk |
| 1 1/2 cups unbleached white flour | 1/4 cup canola oil |
| 1 tablespoon baking powder | 1 egg |
| 1/2 teaspoon sea salt | 1 teaspoon vanilla extract |
| 2 teaspoons ground cinnamon | |

## Goodies

1 cup coarsely chopped roasted walnuts
1 cup coarsely chopped roasted sunflower seeds
12 heaping teaspoons soy margarine or butter
12 heaping teaspoons Sucanat or brown sugar

1. Preheat oven to 375°.

2. Measure and sift the dry ingredients together in a large bowl. Sift a second time. Set aside.

3. Combine the walnuts and sunflower seeds in a small bowl. Add 1 cup of the mixture to the dry ingredients and toss. Retain 1 cup for the topping (see Step 4).

4. Prepare the muffin tins by placing 1 heaping teaspoon soy margarine or butter into each cup. Then sprinkle 1 heaping teaspoon Sucanat or brown sugar in each cup. Finally, sprinkle 2 heaping teaspoons of the chopped walnuts and sunflower seed mixture in each cup. (If you are using jumbo muffin tins, put 2 heaping teaspoons of soy margarine or butter, 2 heaping teaspoons Sucanat or brown sugar, and 4 heaping teaspoons chopped walnuts and sunflower seed in each cup.)

5. Whisk the wet ingredients in a small bowl or blend them in your food processor using the purée blade.

6. Pour the wet ingredients into the dry ingredients. Stir just until mixed. *Do not overstir.*

7. Spoon the batter into greased or papered baking tins. Do not fill the baking tins as full as you would for other muffins.

8. Bake for 15–20 minutes for regular muffins or 20–25 minutes for jumbo.

9. When the muffins are done, immediately turn them upside-down on a platter or baking sheet; *do not remove from the muffin tin.* Allow the muffins to cool in this position for at least 10 minutes. Remove the muffin tin. (You may need the help of a knife to free the *Cinnamon Sticky Muffins.*)

**Serving suggestions:** Serve these as soon as you can after baking or reheat them before serving. Sliced apples or pears and spice tea are a great accompaniment for *Cinnamon Sticky Muffins.*

# Classic Colada Muffins

*Do you remember your first piña colada? Who doesn't? Mine was on the beach in Acapulco. It was the morning after I had danced the hustle all night at a thatched-hut discoteque called the Junkanoo. My new Mexican friend and I were relaxing on the beach, wondering what could possibly top a night like that, when along came an Indian woman, dragging a sack full of fresh coconuts. With a formidable machete in one hand and what looked like a wineskin full of rum in the other, she hailed: "Coco Loco! Coco Loco!" You guessed it. She used the machete to lop off the top of the coconut. Then she poured out a little of the coconut milk and added a hefty shot of rum. That was "Coco Loco."*

*"You forgot the pineapple juice," you say. No. No. No. We had a flask of pineapple juice in our cooler!*

*These muffins capture that wonderful blend of tropical flavors right down to the rum.*

*P. S. It has been my experience that fresh pineapple is too acidic for baking. These muffins work best with canned chopped pineapple (packed in its own juice) that has been well drained. You can use up to 1/2 cup of the drained juice in place of the 1/2 cup of apple juice concentrate to give added pineapple flavor.*

**Yield:** *12 muffins*

| Dry Ingredients | Wet Ingredients |
| --- | --- |
| 1 1/2 cups whole-wheat pastry flour | 3/4 cup apple juice concentrate |
| 1 cup whole-wheat flour | 1 cup soy or cow's milk |
| 1/2 cup unbleached white flour | 1/4 cup canola oil |
| 2 teaspoons baking powder | 2 teaspoons rum extract |
| 1 teaspoon baking soda | |
| 1/2 teaspoon sea salt | |

| Goodies | Topping |
| --- | --- |
| 1/4 cup coconut<br>3/4 cup crushed pineapple,<br>  well drained | 1/4 cup coconut (approximate) |

1. Preheat oven to 400°.

2. Measure and sift the dry ingredients together in a large bowl. Sift a second time. Set aside.

3. Whisk the wet ingredients in a medium bowl or blend them in your food processor using the purée blade.

4. Add the goodies to the wet ingredients and stir to combine.

5. Pour the wet ingredients into the dry ingredients. Stir just until mixed. *Do not overstir.*

6. Spoon the batter into greased or papered baking tins. Fill each cup nearly to the top.

7. Top each muffin with a pinch of coconut.

8. Bake for 15–20 minutes.

9. Cool in the baking tins for at least 10 minutes.

**Serving suggestions:** These make an impressive presentation "straight up" on your favorite dessert plate.

# Dad's Summer Squash Muffins

My dad used to grow peppers, tomatoes, and squash in a garden large enough for a healthy supply of at least six more vegetables. As you can imagine, by the middle of summer we were up to our ears in zucchini and summer squash. My mom, my five sisters, and I were always searching for new and interesting ways to cook with it. We added zucchini to Italian tomato sauce, baked zucchini breads, made puréed squash soups, canned sweet zucchini pickles, and put squash on pasta and in casseroles.

During the summer that I worked on this book, I decided to create a squash muffin. Mmm. Mmm. Try mixing yellow squash and zucchini, half and half. This produces a colorful as well as delicious muffin that is great for dessert and breakfast, too.

**Yield:** *12 muffins*

| Dry Ingredients | Wet Ingredients |
|---|---|
| 1 1/2 cups whole-wheat pastry flour | 1 cup soy or cow's milk |
| 1 cup whole-wheat flour | 1/2 cup canola oil |
| 1/2 cup unbleached white flour | 1/4 cup honey, warmed |
| 2 teaspoons baking powder | 1 tablespoon molasses, warmed |
| 1 teaspoon baking soda | 1 egg |
| 1/4 teaspoon sea salt | |
| 1 teaspoon ground cinnamon | |

## Goodies

1 cup grated yellow squash and/or zucchini
1 cup coarsely chopped roasted walnuts
1 cup raisins

1. Preheat oven to 400°.

2. Measure and sift the dry ingredients together in a large bowl. Sift a second time. Set aside.

3. Add the goodies to the dry ingredients and toss.

4. Whisk the wet ingredients in a small bowl or blend them in your food processor using the purée blade.

5. Pour the wet ingredients into the dry ingredients. Stir just until mixed. *Do not overstir.*

6. Spoon the batter into greased or papered baking tins. Fill each cup nearly to the top.

7. Bake for 15–20 minutes.

8. Cool in the baking tins for at least 10 minutes. Remove from the tins and brush the top of each muffin with canola oil.

**Serving suggestions:** Serve these as you would zucchini bread—sliced with a little soy margarine (or butter) or with whipped cream cheese.

# Glazed Ginger Carrot Muffins

One of my favorite vegetables is carrots glazed with ginger and honey. I lightly steam the carrot slices with grated ginger and then top with honey and margarine just prior to serving. People always want to know what magic I performed. "Just ginger and honey," I reply. "Just ginger and honey."

I've re-created this fabulous combination in my Glazed Ginger Carrot Muffins. No longer relegated to the vegetable department, these carrots with ginger and honey make a scrumptious dessert!

*Yield: 12 muffins*

| Dry Ingredients | Goodies |
|---|---|
| 1 3/4 cups whole-wheat pastry flour | 1 cup grated carrots |
| 1 cup whole-wheat flour | 1 1/2 tablespoons grated ginger |
| 1/2 cup brown-rice flour | root (or 3/4 tablespoon |
| 2 teaspoons baking powder | powdered ginger) |
| 1 teaspoon baking soda | |
| 1/2 teaspoon sea salt | |

| Wet Ingredients | Topping |
|---|---|
| 1/2 cup orange juice concentrate | Orange Glaze (see Gloria's |
| 1 1/4 cups soy or cow's milk | Glorious Glazes on page 168.) |
| 1/4 cup canola oil | |
| 1 egg | |

1. Preheat oven to 400°.

2. Measure and sift the dry ingredients together in a large bowl. Sift a second time. Set aside.

3. Whisk the wet ingredients in a medium bowl or blend them in your food processor using the purée blade.

4. Add the goodies to the wet ingredients and stir to combine.

5. Pour the wet ingredients into the dry ingredients. Stir just until mixed. *Do not overstir.*

6. Spoon the batter into greased or papered baking tins. Fill each cup nearly to the top.

7. Bake for 15–20 minutes.

8. While the muffins bake, prepare the *Orange Glaze*.

9. When the muffins are done, cool them for about 15 minutes in the baking tins. Remove from the tins and coat each muffin with enough glaze to cover the top surface. Cool for an additional 10 minutes before you dig in.


**Serving suggestions:** The warmer the better. Serve these as soon as you can after baking or reheat them before serving.

# Gloria's Glorious Glazes

## Citrus Honey Glaze

**Yield:** *approximately 1/2 cup*

1 tablespoon cornstarch
1/2 cup lemonade or orange juice
1/4 cup honey
1/2 teaspoon grated lemon or orange rind

1. Dissolve the cornstarch in the lemonade or orange juice.

2. Combine the mixture with the honey and citrus rind in a small saucepan.

3. Heat until the mixture begins to boil. Reduce heat.

4. Cook until the glaze thickens and clears, stirring constantly.

5. Remove from heat.

6. After cooling muffins and removing from the tins, glaze the top of each muffin individually.

## Orange Glaze

**Yield:** *approximately 1/2 cup*

1 tablespoon cornstarch
1/4 cup orange juice
3 tablespoons soy margarine or butter
3 tablespoons honey

1. Dissolve the cornstarch in the orange juice.

2. Melt the soy margarine or butter in a small saucepan over medium heat.

3. Add the honey and the cornstarch mixture.

4. Cook until the glaze thickens and clears, stirring constantly.

5. Remove from heat.

6. After cooling muffins and removing from the tins, glaze the top of each muffin individually.

# Sucanat or Brown Sugar Glaze

*Yield: approximately 1/2 cup*

5 tablespoons soy margarine or butter

3 tablespoons Sucanat or brown sugar

1. Melt soy margarine or butter in a small saucepan.

2. Add Sucanat or brown sugar.

3. Stir over low heat until the Sucanat or brown sugar is melted and the consistency is smooth.

4. Remove from heat.

5. After cooling muffins and removing from the tins, glaze the top of each muffin individually.

# Lemon Pecan Muffins

When I visit my Mom, she asks if I have any special requests. "Make a lemon pecan cake," I plead. But since mom's in Pennsylvania and I'm in North Carolina, I only visit twice each year, and so I don't get lemon pecan cake as often as I would like. I created my Lemon Pecan Muffins so I could enjoy that scrumptious combination more often.

Now when I visit my friends, I ask if they have any special requests. "Make us your Lemon Pecan Muffins," they plead.

**Yield:** 12 muffins

| Dry Ingredients | Wet Ingredients |
|---|---|
| 1 1/2 cups whole-wheat flour | 1/2 cup apple juice |
| 1 1/2 cups unbleached white flour | 1 cup soy or cow's milk |
| 1 tablespoon baking powder | 1/4 cup canola oil |
| 1/2 teaspoon sea salt | 1 egg |
| | 3/4 cup all-fruit apricot jam |
| | 3 tablespoons grated lemon rind |

| Goodies |
|---|
| 1 1/2 cups coarsely chopped roasted pecans |

1. Preheat oven to 400°.

2. Measure and sift the dry ingredients together in a large bowl. Sift a second time. Set aside.

3. Add 1 cup of the goodies (chopped pecans) to the dry ingredients and toss. Retain the remaining 1/2 cup for the topping (see Step 7).

4. Whisk the wet ingredients in a small bowl or blend them in your food processor using the purée blade.

5. Pour the wet ingredients into the dry ingredients. Stir just until mixed. *Do not overstir.*

6. Spoon the batter into greased or papered baking tins. Fill each cup nearly to the top.

7. Top each muffin with 2 teaspoons chopped pecans. Lightly press the pecans down into the muffin batter so they will not burn while baking.

8. Bake for 15–20 minutes.

9. Cool in the baking tins for at least 10 minutes.


**Serving suggestions:** These have a light and gentle flavor. They make a great closing to any meal.

# Lyman's Chocolate Cheesecake Muffins

*Getting a master's degree was the hardest thing I ever did (before I took up meditation, that is!). I returned to school after an eleven-year absence, most of which time I had worked professionally as a bureaucrat. I was not in the habit of studying. The task would have been impossible had it not been for my friends Lyman, Susan, and Jim. We'd get together regularly to blow off steam, usually over a great meal.*

*Lyman was in the habit of dazzling us with his scrumptious desserts. He often made a chocolate cheesecake that knocked our socks off. I believe I have done justice to this wonder with my Lyman's Chocolate Cheesecake Muffins.*

*Yes, it is chocolate—but with no refined sugar. I buy naturally sweetened chocolate chips at my local health-food store. They are sweetened with barley malt instead of refined sugar.*

*Of course, if you prefer carob to chocolate, make these muffins by substituting carob powder for the cocoa and carob chips for the naturally sweetened chocolate chips. Carob has a flavor similar to chocolate but contains less fat and no caffeine. By the way, if you toast the carob powder, it becomes even richer.*

**Yield:** *14 muffins*

| Dry Ingredients | Wet Ingredients |
| --- | --- |
| 2 1/2 cups whole-wheat pastry flour | 8 ounces cream cheese, softened |
| 2 teaspoons baking powder | 1/2 cup low-fat sour cream |
| 1 teaspoon baking soda | 1 cup apple juice |
| 1/2 teaspoon sea salt | 1 egg |
| 1/2 cup cocoa powder | 1/2 cup honey, warmed |
| | 2 teaspoons vanilla extract |

## Goodies

1 1/4 cups naturally sweetened chocolate chips

1. Preheat oven to 400°.
2. Measure and sift the dry ingredients together in a large bowl. Sift a second time.
3. Add the goodies to the dry ingredients and toss. Set aside.
4. Using the purée blade of your food processor, cream the cream cheese and sour cream. Add the remaining wet ingredients and blend. (If you do not have a food processor, use a hand-held mixer at medium speed.)
5. Pour the wet ingredients into the dry ingredients. Stir just until mixed. *Do not overstir.*
6. Spoon the batter into greased or papered baking tins. Fill each cup nearly to the top.
7. Bake for 15–20 minutes.
8. Cool in the baking tins for at least 10 minutes. Remove from the tins and brush the top of each muffin with canola oil.

*Serving suggestions:* Slice *Lyman's Chocolate Cheesecake Muffins* into four or five slices and fan the slices on your favorite dessert plate. Top with fresh bing cherries or sliced fresh strawberries and (if your diet allows) garnish with a dollop of whipped cream or low-fat sour cream and a sprinkling of chocolate or carob chips.

# Mocha Chip Muffins

*When I lived in Virginia Beach, my friends Jake and Lila and I often biked over to High's Ice Cream Parlor for an afternoon snack. While Jake usually ordered a spritzer float (lemon soda with fruit sherbet), and Lila, an ice cream cone, I asked for a chocolate shake blended with a teaspoon of instant coffee. Mmm. Mmm. The coffee granules dissolved in the shake, turning the rich chocolate flavor into a mocha delight. The three of us hummed all the way home.*

*Well, I'm humming again over the combination of coffee and chocolate in my Mocha Chip Muffins.*

**Yield:** *12 muffins*

| Dry Ingredients | Wet Ingredients |
|---|---|
| 1 cup whole-wheat pastry flour | 1 1/2 cups triple strength |
| 1 cup whole-wheat flour | coffee, cooled |
| 1/2 cup unbleached white flour | 1/4 cup canola oil |
| 1 tablespoon baking powder | 1/4 cup butter, melted |
| 1/2 teaspoon sea salt | 1 egg |
| 1/2 cup Sucanat or brown sugar | 2 teaspoons vanilla extract |

### Goodies

1 cup coarsely chopped roasted walnuts
1 1/4 cups naturally sweetened chocolate chips

1. Preheat oven to 400°.

2. Measure and sift the dry ingredients together in a large bowl. Sift a second time. Set aside.

3. Add the goodies to the dry ingredients and toss.

4. Whisk the wet ingredients in a small bowl or purée them in your food processor using the purée blade.

5. Pour the wet ingredients into the dry ingredients. Stir just until mixed. *Do not overstir.*

6. Spoon the batter into greased or papered baking tins. Fill each cup nearly to the top.

7. Bake for 15–20 minutes.

8. Cool in the baking tins for at least 10 minutes. Remove from the tins and brush the top of each muffin with canola oil.

*Serving suggestions:* I like to serve these warm—topped with a scoop of vanilla ice cream or frozen yogurt. Try icing them with your favorite vanilla icing.

# Mom's Applesauce Muffins

*Mom's back, but this time with her bridge party applesauce cake. Always a crowd-pleaser, mom's applesauce cake is like a rich, dark, apple pound-cake. Guests marvel at the unique combination of flavors.*

*Try this muffin adaptation of my mom's cake recipe and you will see that it's in a class all its own. Maybe it's the touch of cocoa that sets it apart. Or maybe it's the dates. I don't know. But I do know that you are going to love these muffins.*

*P.S. Save yourself some time and buy the dates already chopped.*

**Yield:** *12 muffins*

| Dry Ingredients | Wet Ingredients |
| --- | --- |
| 1 1/2 cups whole-wheat pastry flour | 1 cup chunky applesauce |
| 1 cup whole-wheat flour | 3/4 cup apple juice |
| 2 teaspoons baking powder | 1/2 cup soy or cow's milk |
| 1 teaspoon baking soda | 1/4 cup canola oil |
| 1/2 teaspoon sea salt | 1 egg |
| 1 teaspoon cocoa | |
| 1 teaspoon ground cinnamon | |
| 1/2 teaspoon ground nutmeg | |
| 1/2 teaspoon ground allspice | |

### Goodies

3/4 cup coarsely chopped roasted walnuts
3/4 cup chopped dates
3/4 cup raisins

# DESSERT MUFFINS

1. Preheat oven to 400°.

2. Measure and sift the dry ingredients together in a large bowl. Sift a second time. Set aside.

3. Whisk the wet ingredients in a medium bowl or blend them in your food processor using the purée blade and place them in a medium bowl.

4. Add the goodies to the wet ingredients and stir to combine.

5. Pour the wet ingredients into the dry ingredients. Stir just until mixed. *Do not overstir.*

6. Spoon the batter into greased or papered baking tins. Fill each cup nearly to the top.

7. Bake for 15–20 minutes.

8. Cool in the baking tins for at least 10 minutes. Remove from the tins and brush the top of each muffin with canola oil.

*Serving suggestions:* Enjoy these plain or with whipped cream cheese, and experience oneness with the universe.

# Only-Kids-Need-Apply Muffins

*If it weren't for peanut butter, I would not be alive today. Sound familiar? If so, you will love my Only-Kids-Need-Apply Muffins.*

*As for the carob . . . For those of you who are unfamiliar with it, carob is a naturally sweet food that is similar to chocolate in flavor but with less fat and only about half the calories. And it does not contain caffeine. Is it a substitute for chocolate? Not really, and it is probably best not to think of carob in those terms. It has a flavor all its own.*

*Be aware that carob chips usually are not dairy-free. Ask your health-food-store clerk about the products you plan to buy.*

**Yield:** *12 muffins*

| Dry Ingredients | Wet Ingredients |
| --- | --- |
| 1 cup whole-wheat pastry flour | 1 cup hot water |
| 1 cup whole-wheat flour | 1/2 cup chunky peanut butter |
| 1/2 cup unbleached white flour | 1 cup soy or cow's milk |
| 1/4 cup toasted wheat germ | 1/4 cup canola oil |
| 2 teaspoons baking powder | 1/4 cup honey, warmed |
| 1 teaspoon baking soda | |

| Goodies |
| --- |
| 1 1/4 cups carob chips |

1. Preheat oven to 400°.

2. Measure and sift the dry ingredients together in a large bowl. Sift a second time. Set aside.

3. Add the goodies to the dry ingredients and toss.

4. Using the purée blade of your food processor, blend the wet ingredients. (If you do not have a food processor, stir the peanut butter and hot water together in a small bowl until they have a smooth consistency. Add the milk, oil, and honey to the peanut butter mixture and blend thoroughly.)

5. Pour the wet ingredients into the dry ingredients. Stir just until mixed. *Do not overstir.*

6. Spoon the batter into greased or papered baking tins. Fill each cup nearly to the top.

7. Bake for 15–20 minutes.

8. Cool in the baking tins for at least 10 minutes. Remove from the tins and brush the top of each muffin with canola oil.

**Serving suggestions:** If you are feeling particularly wicked, cut these into four or five slices and fan the slices on a plate. Place a scoop of vanilla ice cream or frozen yogurt alongside the slices. Sprinkle with coconut.

# Orange Cardamom Muffins

*Cardamom is that wonderful spice that gives coffee cakes and danish pastries their distinctive flavor. It is native to India but is cultivated and used extensively throughout Southeast Asia in curries, cakes, and spiced teas. Cardamom is probably my favorite spice, and I expect these muffins will show you why.*

*You can buy pre-packaged slivered almonds for this recipe. It doesn't make sense to try to sliver them yourself.*

**Yield:** *12 muffins*

| Dry Ingredients | Wet Ingredients |
|---|---|
| 1 1/2 cups whole-wheat pastry flour | 3/4 cup orange juice concentrate |
| 1 1/2 cups whole-wheat flour | 1 cup soy or cow's milk |
| 1/2 cup unbleached white flour | 1/4 cup canola oil |
| 2 teaspoons baking powder | 1 egg |
| 1 teaspoon baking soda | 1/2 cup honey, warmed |
| 1/2 teaspoon sea salt | 2 tablespoons grated orange rind |
| 1 1/4 teaspoons ground cardamom | |

| Topping |
|---|
| 3/4 cup slivered almonds |

1. Preheat oven to 400°.

2. Measure and sift the dry ingredients together in a large bowl. Sift a second time. Set aside.

3. Whisk the wet ingredients in a small bowl or blend them in your food processor using the purée blade.

4. Pour the wet ingredients into the dry ingredients. Stir just until mixed. *Do not overstir.*

5. Spoon the batter into greased or papered baking tins. Fill each cup nearly to the top.

6. Top each muffin with 2 teaspoons slivered almonds.

7. Bake for 15–20 minutes.

8. Cool in the baking tins for at least 10 minutes. Remove from the tins and brush the top of each muffin with canola oil.

**Serving suggestions:** Cut *Orange Cardamom Muffins* into four or five slices, fan the slices on a dessert plate, and drizzle with *Vanilla Custard Sauce* (see *Gloria's Glorious Muffin Sauces* on page 152).

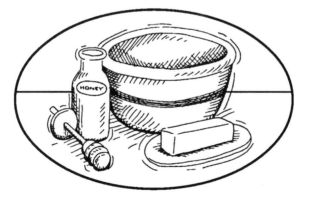

# Orange Poppy Seed Muffins

*Poppy seeds can be quite expensive if you buy commercial brands at your local food store. If you buy them in bulk from food co-ops and even health-food stores, they are about one-fourth the price. And they keep very well.*

*If you want to give these muffins an extra burst of poppy seed flavor, grind the seeds with a mortar and pestle, whirl them in your food processor using the purée blade, or go high tech with an electric spice mill.*

*Notice that the only sweetener in the muffin itself is the all-fruit marmalade. Extra sweetness is poured on after the muffins bake and before they drive you wild.*

**Yield:** *12 muffins*

| Dry Ingredients | Wet Ingredients |
| --- | --- |
| 2 1/2 cups whole-wheat pastry flour | 1 1/2 cups orange juice |
| 1 cup whole-wheat flour | 1/4 cup canola oil |
| 1 tablespoon baking powder | 1 egg |
| 1/2 teaspoon sea salt | 1/2 cup all-fruit orange marmalade |
| 1/4 cup poppy seeds | 3 tablespoons grated orange rind |

| Topping |
| --- |
| Orange Glaze (see Gloria's Glorious Glazes on page 168) |

1. Preheat oven to 375°.

2. Measure and sift all the dry ingredients *except the poppy seeds* together in a large bowl. Sift a second time. Add the poppy seeds and toss. Set aside.

3. Whisk the wet ingredients in a small bowl or blend them in your food processor using the purée blade.

4. Pour the wet ingredients into the dry ingredients. Stir just until mixed. *Do not overstir.*

5. Spoon the batter into greased or papered baking tins. Fill each cup nearly to the top.

6. Bake for 15–20 minutes.

7. While the muffins bake, prepare the *Orange Glaze*.

8. When the muffins are done, remove them from the oven and immediately poke three or four holes in each muffin using a toothpick or skewer. Drizzle the warm glaze over the top of each muffin so that the glaze can soak through the muffin.

9. Cool for 10 minutes before removing muffins from the baking tins.

**Serving suggestions:** These stand alone.

# Peachy Peach Muffins

*This is essentially the same recipe as Thanks-to-the-Tropical-Sun Muffins (see page 86) but has the advantage of using a fruit that is less expensive and more commonly available. When fresh peaches are out of season, you can use canned peaches (packed in fruit juice).*

*The dried peaches are available at both health-food stores and food co-ops. They also are packaged commercially by several major fruit-preserving companies so you may find them in your regular grocery store next to the raisins and prunes.*

**Yield:** *12 muffins*

| Dry Ingredients | Wet Ingredients |
|---|---|
| 1 cup whole-wheat pastry flour | 1/2 cup canola oil |
| 3/4 cup whole-wheat flour | 1 egg |
| 1 cup unbleached white flour | 1/2 cup peach all-fruit jam |
| 2 teaspoons baking powder | 1/2 teaspoon rum extract |
| 1 teaspoon baking soda | 1 teaspoon grated orange rind |
| 1/2 teaspoon sea salt | |

| Goodies |
|---|
| 1 1/2 cups fresh peaches or a 1-pound can |
| of peaches packed in fruit juice, well drained |
| 1 cup chopped dried peaches |

1. Preheat oven to 400°.

2. Measure and sift the dry ingredients together in a large bowl. Sift a second time. Set aside.

3. Whisk the wet ingredients in a medium bowl or blend them in your food processor using the purée blade and place them in a medium bowl.

4. Using the purée blade of your food processor, purée the fresh or canned peaches. (If you do not have a food processor, mash the peaches by hand using a fork or a potato ricer.) Measure and add the puréed peaches to the wet ingredients. Add the remaining goody ingredient (dried peaches) and stir to combine.

5. Pour the wet ingredients into the dry ingredients. Stir just until mixed. *Do not overstir.*

6. Spoon the batter into greased or papered baking tins. Fill each cup nearly to the top.

7. Bake for 15–20 minutes.

8. Cool in the baking tins for at least 10 minutes. Remove from the tins and brush the top of each muffin with canola oil.

*Serving suggestions:* I love it when peaches, cantaloupe, and blueberries come into season together, don't you? Why try to improve on nature? Make *Peachy Peach Muffins* when the peaches are at peak and serve them with blueberries and cantaloupe.

# Raspberry Bouquet Muffins

*When it comes to berries, raspberries are the upper crust. They exude their specialness into everything they touch. My Raspberry Bouquet Muffins are no exception.*

*When working with raspberries, remember that they tend to lack the firmness of other berries, and they can go all to pieces when baked. Take care to select the firmest berries you can find for Raspberry Bouquet Muffins.*

*When raspberries are not in season, use frozen raspberries (see Step 3). I have only been able to find frozen raspberries packed in light syrup. For lack of a sugarless variety, I have used these. Buy two 10-ounce packages.*

**Yield:** *16–18 muffins*

| Dry Ingredients | Wet Ingredients |
| --- | --- |
| 3 cups whole-wheat pastry flour | 1/2 cup apple juice concentrate |
| 1/2 cup unbleached white flour | 3/4 cup buttermilk |
| 2 teaspoons baking powder | 1/4 cup canola oil |
| 1 teaspoon baking soda | 1 egg |
| 1/2 teaspoon sea salt | 1 cup all-fruit raspberry jam |
| | 2 teaspoons vanilla extract |
| | 2 teaspoons grated lemon rind |

| Goodies |
| --- |
| 1 1/4 cups fresh or frozen raspberries |

1. Preheat oven to 375°.

2. Measure and sift the dry ingredients together in a large bowl. Sift a second time. Set aside.

3. Wash the berries. Remove any stems and leaves. Select 1 1/4 cups of the firmest berries. Add the raspberries to the dry ingredients and toss to coat them with flour. This will keep them from bleeding into the rest of the muffin. (If you are using frozen berries, drain the berries very well before adding them to the dry ingredients. If you like, substitute up to 1/2 cup of the drained liquid for up to 1/2 cup of apple juice concentrate. Be aware that your muffins will be red if you make this substitution.)

4. Whisk the wet ingredients in a small bowl or blend them in your food processor using the purée blade.

5. Pour the wet ingredients into the dry ingredients. Stir just until mixed. *Do not overstir.*

6. Spoon the batter into greased or papered baking tins. Fill each cup nearly to the top.

7. Bake for 15–20 minutes.

8. Cool in the baking tins for at least 10 minutes. Remove from the tins and brush the top of each muffin with canola oil.


**Serving suggestions:** There are many ways to enjoy these muffins. For a light palate pleaser, try them with lemon sherbet or sorbet. Or slice them in half, top each half with vanilla ice cream and hot all-fruit raspberry jam. If you are feeling totally outrageous, serve *Raspberry Bouquet Muffins* with a drizzle of warm *Chocolate-Raspberry Custard Sauce* (see *Gloria's Glorious Muffin Sauces* on page 153).

# Seven-Factors-of-Enlightenment Muffins

*In Buddhism, there are seven factors or states of mind that must be cultivated and be present in the heart in order for enlightenment to arise. These are mindfulness, investigation, effort, rapture, concentration, tranquility, and equanimity. Meditators work to both strengthen these states of mind when they occur and free the heart from the states of mind that obstruct them. I developed these muffins to honor this skillful undertaking.*

*The Seven-Factors-of-Enlightenment Muffins include seven wonderful ingredients—applesauce, carob chips, coconut, granola, honey, sunflower seeds, and walnuts. Try them and discover their enlightening qualities.*

**Yield:** *18 muffins*

| Dry Ingredients | Wet Ingredients |
| --- | --- |
| 1 cup whole-wheat pastry flour | 1/2 cup applesauce |
| 1 cup whole-wheat flour | 1 1/4 cups soy or cow's milk |
| 1/2 cup unbleached white flour | 1/4 cup canola oil |
| 2 teaspoons baking powder | 1 egg |
| 1/2 teaspoon baking soda | 2 teaspoons vanilla extract |
| 1/2 cup Sucanat or brown sugar | |
| 1/4 teaspoon sea salt | |
| 1/2 teaspoon ground cinnamon | |

| Goodies | |
| --- | --- |
| 1/2 cup coarsely chopped roasted walnuts | 3/4 cup carob chips |
| | 1/2 cup shredded coconut |
| 3/4 cup granola | 3/4 cup roasted sunflower seeds |

## Topping

1/4 cup coconut (approximate)

1. Preheat oven to 400°.
2. Measure and sift the dry ingredients together in a large bowl. Sift a second time. Set aside.
3. Add the goodies to the dry ingredients and toss.
4. Whisk the wet ingredients in a small bowl or blend them in your food processor using the purée blade.
5. Pour the wet ingredients into the dry ingredients. Stir just until mixed. *Do not overstir.*
6. Spoon the batter into greased or papered baking tins. Fill each cup nearly to the top.
7. Top each muffin with a pinch of coconut.
8. Bake for 15–20 minutes.
9. Cool in the baking tins for at least 10 minutes.

**Serving suggestions:** I love a cup of dark-roast coffee with these.

# Strawberry Muffins

*I love the way the English use custard sauce. It is quite common for them to pour custard sauce over fresh fruit, baked apples, pound cake, or even pudding! During my first week in England, I ordered bread-and-butter pudding at a tea shop. The pudding was served with fresh strawberries, a warm vanilla custard sauce, and a daub of clotted cream. "This is perfection," I thought. "I always knew the English were a sensible lot, but this confirms it."*

*My Strawberry Muffins are triple-rich with strawberry goodness. They include fresh strawberries, strawberry jam, and strawberry extract. Topped with my Vanilla Custard Sauce, they are a match for English pudding and definitely something to write home about.*

**Yield:** *12 muffins*

| Dry Ingredients | Wet Ingredients |
|---|---|
| 1 1/4 cups whole-wheat pastry flour | 1 egg |
| 1 cup whole-wheat flour | 1 cup all-fruit strawberry jam |
| 1 cup unbleached white flour | 2 teaspoons grated lemon rind |
| 2 teaspoons baking powder | 1 teaspoon vanilla extract |
| 1 teaspoon baking soda | 3 teaspoons strawberry extract |
| 1/2 teaspoon sea salt | |
| 1/8 teaspoon mace | |

### Goodies

1 pint fresh strawberries (approximate)

1. Preheat oven to 400°.

2. Measure and sift the dry ingredients together in a large bowl. Sift a second time. Set aside.

3. Using the purée blade of your food processor, purée the fresh strawberries until they are smooth. (If you do not have a food processor, a blender will work just as well.) Remove the puréed strawberries from the food processor (blender), measure 1 1/2 cups, and place them in a medium bowl.

4. Whisk the wet ingredients in a small bowl or blend them in your food processor using the purée blade. Add the wet ingredients to the strawberries.

5. Pour the wet ingredients into the dry ingredients. Stir just until mixed. *Do not overstir.*

6. Spoon the batter into greased or papered baking tins. Fill each cup nearly to the top.

7. Bake for 15–20 minutes.

8. Cool in the baking tins for at least 10 minutes. Remove from the tins and brush the top of each muffin with canola oil.

**Serving suggestions:** Cut warm muffins into four or five slices and fan them out on a dessert plate. Top each serving with a large spoonful of quartered fresh strawberries and about 1/8 cup *Vanilla Custard Sauce* (see *Gloria's Glorious Muffin Sauces* on page 152). Or cut the muffins in half and place a slice or scoop of non-fat frozen vanilla yogurt on the bottom half. Replace the top half and drizzle with *Vanilla Custard Sauce.* Awesome!

# HOLIDAY MUFFINS

*For now I am in a holiday humour.*
William Shakespeare,
*As You Like It,* Act IV, Scene i

I am rarely without an excuse to bake muffins; breathing is excuse enough. But, as you can imagine, if I bake muffins every time I take a breath, I will feel a tad obsessed before long. That's why I love the holidays. They give me zillions of excuses to bake. Consider:

• The holiday season means parties, lots of parties—office parties, club parties, school parties. My friend Susan loves to bring muffins to parties. She says that muffins are always the most popular offering, and people remember who brought them! (You don't have to limit yourself to the muffin recipes in this section. Susan says all of my muffins are great for parties.)

• Holidays are a time for "drop-in" visits. Bake muffins to have "a little something" to serve unexpected company. Start baking at Halloween and go right on through the New Year. I'll bet you will use every muffin you bake.

• Muffins make wonderful presents—for teachers, family, friends, and holiday hosts. Fill a nicely decorated basket with a dozen muffins. Add a jar of *Gloria's Glorious Muffin Sauces* (see page 152) or a tub of *Gloria's Glorious Muffin Butters and Spreads* (see page 56) and you've got an unforgettable gift.

• Muffins let you "prepare" for unexpected gifts. Keep several dozen muffins (individually wrapped and labeled) in the freezer just in case someone arrives with an unexpected gift for you! I keep an assortment of wicker baskets on hand, and when I need a gift, I have an interesting basket ready to fill with muffins When you give a gift of muffins, why not include a card with instructions for freezing and reheating? (See page 32.)

Whether you make them to stuff stockings or to stuff faces, muffins will be a most welcome holiday treat. And what about the rest of the year? What about the birthdays, un-birthdays, and other holidays? You can bake these festive party muffins for any occasion throughout the year.

# Anise Orange Muffins

Some people say that one has to acquire a taste for anise. Maybe they are right. I never gave it a second thought because, one way or another, anise always has been part of my diet. When I was a teething baby, my mom gave my sisters and me anise-flavored zwieback. This twice-baked bread soothed teething gums and satisfied a youthful sweet tooth.

As I grew older, my love of anise became a devotion to Good 'n Plenty candy, a pink and white sugar-coated licorice, popular at Saturday afternoon movies in New Jersey. Yum-O.

In more recent years, one of my favorite anise sweets has been Biscotti, a chocolate-covered anisette biscuit sold at Italian food markets.

But why Anise Orange Muffins, you ask? Because anise goes great with orange. When it came to creating an anise muffin, I just had to give it a burst of citrus.

**Yield:** 14 muffins

| Dry Ingredients | Wet Ingredients |
| --- | --- |
| 1 3/4 cups whole-wheat flour | 1/2 cup orange juice concentrate |
| 1 3/4 cups unbleached white flour | 1 cup low-fat cottage cheese |
| 2 teaspoons baking powder | 1/2 cup soy or cow's milk |
| 1 teaspoon baking soda | 1/2 cup canola oil |
| 1/2 teaspoon sea salt | 1 egg |
| 1/2 teaspoon ground cardamom | 1/2 cup honey, warmed |
| | 1 tablespoon grated orange rind |

| Goodies |
| --- |
| 2 1/2 tablespoons anise seeds |

1. Preheat oven to 400°.

2. Measure and sift the dry ingredients together in a large bowl. Sift a second time. Set aside.

3. Using a mortar and pestle, the purée blade of your food processor, or an electric spice mill, grind the anise seeds. (This will bring forth their wonderful flavor.) Add the seeds to the dry ingredients and toss.

4. Whisk the wet ingredients in a medium bowl. *Do not use a blender or food processor.*

5. Pour the wet ingredients into the dry ingredients. Stir just until mixed. *Do not overstir.*

6. Spoon the batter into greased or papered baking tins. Fill each cup nearly to the top.

7. Bake for 15–20 minutes.

8. Cool in the baking tins for at least 10 minutes. Remove from the tins and brush the top of each muffin with canola oil.


**Serving suggestions:** I put *Anise Orange Muffins* in the holiday chapter of *Gloria's Glorious Muffins* because they go great with winter-holiday meals. Needless to say, however, you can enjoy them year round. Try my *Anise Orange Muffins* plain or with a drizzle of *Chocolate Fudge Sauce* (see *Gloria's Glorious Muffins Sauces* on page 154) and, if you dare, a squirt of light whipped cream.

# Blackberry Cheesecake Muffins

Once upon a time, cheesecake was a simple dessert made from soft cheeses and served plain—just plain. Remember that? When it first became popular, we didn't add much to it or swirl things through it. We enjoyed it plain—with a side of coffee or tea.

Before long, however, we discovered the remarkable versatility of cheesecake. We daubed it with blueberries, cherries, and pineapples. Then we laced it with Amaretto or brandy, layered it with raspberry conserve, and topped it with kiwi and star fruit. It was a veritable cheesecake explosion!

It was only a matter of time before someone put blackberries and cheesecake together. "Pure inspiration," I thought when I first tasted that combination. "I've got to create a blackberry cheesecake muffin for the holidays." This is a great holiday muffin that will be a real crowd-pleaser. I guarantee it.

As with the Chocolate-Covered Cherry Muffins, I anticipated the difficulty of finding fresh blackberries in winter and use frozen blackberries packaged in 12-ounce freezer bags.

**Yield:** 14–16 muffins

| Dry Ingredients | Wet Ingredients |
| --- | --- |
| 2 cups whole-wheat pastry flour | 8 ounces cream cheese, softened |
| 1/2 cup unbleached white flour | 1/2 cup low-fat sour cream |
| 2 teaspoons baking powder | 1 egg |
| 1 teaspoon baking soda | 1 teaspoon vanilla extract |
| 1/2 cup Sucanat or brown sugar | 1 teaspoon rum extract |
| 1/2 teaspoon sea salt | 1 teaspoon grated lemon rind |
| 1/4 teaspoon ground nutmeg | |

**Goodies**

12-ounce package frozen blackberries (about 1 1/2 cups)

1. Place the bag of frozen blackberries in a large bowl of very hot water for at least 20 minutes or follow the microwave defrosting instructions on the package.

2. Preheat oven to 400°.

3. Measure and sift the dry ingredients together in a large bowl. Sift a second time. Set aside.

4. Using the purée blade of your food processor, cream the cream cheese and sour cream. Add the remaining wet ingredients and blend. (If you do not have a food processor, use a hand-held mixer at medium speed.) Place the wet ingredients in a medium bowl.

5. Using the purée blade of your food processor, chop the blackberries as follows: Empty the bag of thawed blackberries into the food processor. Chop the blackberries by pulsing once or twice. *Do not purée.* (If you do not have a food processor, chop the blackberries by hand.) Add the blackberries to the wet ingredients and stir to combine.

6. Pour the wet ingredients into the dry ingredients. Stir just until mixed. *Do not overstir.*

7. Spoon the batter into greased or papered baking tins. Fill each cup nearly to the top.

8. Bake for 15–20 minutes.

9. Cool in the baking tins for at least 10 minutes. Remove from the tins and brush the top of each muffin with canola oil.

**Serving suggestions:** Serve *Blackberry Cheesecake Muffins* with sliced kiwi or star fruit. Why not?

# Charity Nut Muffins

*Charity nut cups are little nut pies made in mini-muffin tins. The tins are lined with pie crust and filled with a delightful blend of nuts, brown sugar, and butter. Mmm. Mmm. Mmm! The nutty, crunchy filling makes them so appealing.*

*I've transformed this wonderful holiday dessert into an equally delightful muffin. And to make it more nutritious, I've laced the nut filling with toasted wheat germ. These will knock your socks off!*

**Yield:** *12 muffins*

| Dry Ingredients | Wet Ingredients |
|---|---|
| 2 cups whole-wheat pastry flour | 1 cup buttermilk |
| 1/2 cup whole-wheat flour | 1/2 cup water |
| 1/2 cup unbleached white flour | 1/4 cup canola oil |
| 1 tablespoon soy flour | 1 egg |
| 2 teaspoons baking powder | 1 teaspoon vanilla extract |
| 1 teaspoon baking soda | 1/2 cup honey, warmed |
| 1/2 teaspoon sea salt | |

## Goodies

1 1/4 cups finely chopped roasted walnuts
1/2 cup toasted wheat germ
1/2 cup Sucanat or brown sugar
1/4 cup soy margarine or butter, melted

1. Preheat oven to 400°.

2. Measure and sift the dry ingredients together in a large bowl. Sift a second time. Set aside.

3. Combine the walnuts, wheat germ, and Sucanat or brown sugar in a small bowl. Retain 1 cup of the mixture to use in a topping (see Step 4) and add the remainder to the dry ingredients. Toss to distribute evenly throughout.

4. Drizzle the melted margarine or butter over the 1 cup of the goodie mixture that you retained in Step 3. Mix to form a crumbly topping. Set aside.

5. Whisk the wet ingredients in a small bowl or blend them in your food processor using the purée blade.

6. Pour the wet ingredients into the dry ingredients. Stir just until mixed. *Do not overstir.*

7. Spoon the batter into greased or papered baking tins filling each tin only about 2/3 full. Leave room for the topping.

8. Generously spoon the goody mixture (Step 4) on top of each muffin. You should use all the mixture on a dozen muffins. (You want to make them nice and crunchy.)

9. Bake for 15–20 minutes.

*Serving suggestions:* If you can afford the saturated fat in your diet, try these sliced and topped with *Honey/Cinnamon Spread* (see *Gloria's Glorious Muffin Butters and Spreads* on page 56). Or enjoy them with your favorite apple butter.

# Chocolate-Covered-Cherry Muffins

The holiday dessert cart is not complete without at least one chocolate selection. Chocolate-Covered-Cherry Muffins are sure to bring smiles to holiday faces. And unlike most chocolate-y treats, these can be made without dairy or refined sugar—use soy milk and naturally sweetened chips that contain no dairy.

It can be difficult to find fresh bing cherries in winter. I anticipated that difficulty and created Chocolate-Covered-Cherry Muffins with frozen dark sweet cherries. The frozen cherries I have seen are sold pitted in 12-ounce freezer bags and are packed without sugar. If you find frozen dark sweet cherries that are packaged differently, use an equivalent portion. As cherries are a tad too large to hold their shape in muffins, I chop them first (see Step 5).

*Yield: 12 muffins*

| Dry Ingredients | Wet Ingredients |
|---|---|
| 1 3/4 cups whole-wheat pastry flour | 3/4 cup soy or cow's milk |
| 1/2 cup unbleached white flour | 1/4 cup canola oil |
| 1 1/2 teaspoons baking powder | 1 egg |
| 1 teaspoon baking soda | 1/2 cup honey, warmed |
| 1/2 teaspoon sea salt | 2 teaspoons vanilla extract |
| 6 tablespoons cocoa powder | |

### Goodies

12-ounce package frozen dark sweet cherries (about 2 cups)
1 cup naturally sweetened chocolate chips

1. Place the bag of frozen cherries in a large bowl of very hot water for at least 20 minutes or follow the microwave defrosting instructions on the package.

2. Preheat oven to 400°.

3. Measure and sift the dry ingredients together in a large bowl. Sift a second time. Set aside.

4. Whisk the wet ingredients in a medium bowl or blend them in your food processor using the purée blade.

5. Using the purée blade of your food processor, chop the cherries as follows: Empty the bag of thawed cherries into the food processor. Chop the cherries by pulsing once or twice. *Do not purée*. (If you do not have a food processor, chop the cherries by hand.) Add the cherries to the wet ingredients. Add the remaining goody ingredient (chocolate chips) to the wet ingredients and stir to combine.

6. Pour the wet ingredients into the dry ingredients. Stir just until mixed. *Do not overstir.*

7. Spoon the batter into greased or papered baking tins. Fill each cup nearly to the top.

8. Bake for 15–20 minutes.

9. Cool in the baking tins for at least 10 minutes. Remove from the tins and brush the top of each muffin with canola oil.

**Serving suggestions:** I doubt that you will want to add anything to these muffins. The chocolate says it all. But you might find a nice hot cup of espresso a dashing accompaniment.

# Cranberry Orange Muffins

*Twenty years ago, my oldest sister, Betty, introduced our family to cranberry nut loaf. My youngest sisters, Barbara and Beverly, remember how dazzled we were to see cranberries in bread! "I thought they only came in cranberry sauce," they said. We loved the flavor, and quickly made cranberry nut loaf a holiday tradition.*

*More recently, I created a cranberry-orange-walnut relish that is fast becoming another tradition. My recipe for Cranberry Orange Muffins is a spin-off of Betty's bread and my relish. Enjoy!*

**Yield:** *12 muffins or 36 mini-muffins*

| Dry Ingredients | Wet Ingredients |
|---|---|
| 2 1/4 cups whole-wheat pastry flour | 1/2 cup apple juice concentrate |
| 1/2 cup unbleached white flour | 1/2 cup soy or cow's milk |
| 2 teaspoons baking powder | 1/4 cup canola oil |
| 1 teaspoon baking soda | 1 egg |
| 1/2 teaspoon sea salt | 1 cup all-fruit orange marmalade |
| | 2 tablespoons grated orange rind |
| | 1 teaspoon vanilla |

| Goodies |
|---|
| 1 cup chopped cranberries |
| 1 cup coarsely chopped roasted walnuts |

1. Preheat oven to 400°.

2. Measure and sift the dry ingredients together in a large bowl. Sift a second time. Set aside.

3. Add the cranberries to the dry ingredients. Toss to coat them with flour. This keeps them from bleeding into the rest of the muffin. Add the remaining goody ingredient (walnuts) to the dry ingredients and toss.

4. Whisk the wet ingredients in a small bowl or blend them in your food processor using the purée blade.

5. Pour the wet ingredients into the dry ingredients. Stir just until mixed. *Do not overstir.*

6. Spoon the batter into greased or papered baking tins. Fill each cup nearly to the top.

7. Bake for 15–20 minutes for regular muffins or 10–15 minutes for mini-muffins.

8. Cool in the baking tins for at least 10 minutes. Remove from the tins and brush the top of each muffin with canola oil.

**Serving suggestions:** You can serve *Cranberry Orange Muffins* with any of your holiday meals or just have them around for breakfast or tea. They are great with whipped cream cheese and orange marmalade.

# Easy-Living Southern Pecan Muffins

*Southerners are proud of their pecans. It's rare to even think of the word "pecan" without "Southern" as a prefix, isn't it? And one of the most-loved recipes for this home-grown product is Southern pecan pie. Holiday dessert carts seem half-dressed without it.*

*I've taken my favorite pecan pie recipe and turned it into unbeatable Easy-Living Southern Pecan Muffins. They are unlike most muffins in that they have a thick, soft Southern pecan topping that oozes into the cake below. Way to go, Dixie!*

*If these are not eaten on the day that you make them (unlikely, but possible), be sure to store them in the refrigerator. The egg topping requires refrigeration.*

*P. S. Because they include more egg and margarine or butter than most of my muffins, Easy-Living Southern Pecan Muffins are higher in cholesterol.*

**Yield:** *12 muffins*

## Dry Ingredients

| | |
|---|---|
| 1 cup whole-wheat pastry flour | 1 teaspoon baking soda |
| 2 cups unbleached white flour | 1/2 teaspoon sea salt |
| 2 teaspoons baking powder | |

## Goodies

| | |
|---|---|
| 1 1/2 cups coarsely chopped pecans | 1/4 cup Sucanat or brown sugar |
| 4 tablespoons soy margarine or butter, melted | 1/4 teaspoon sea salt |
| | 1 egg |
| 1 1/2 teaspoons cornstarch | 1/4 teaspoon vanilla extract |
| 1/2 cup apple juice concentrate | |

# H O L I D A Y   M U F F I N S

---

## Wet Ingredients

| | |
|---|---|
| 1 1/4 cups soy or cow's milk | 1/2 cup honey, warmed |
| 1/2 cup canola oil | 1 1/2 teaspoons vanilla extract |
| 1 egg | |

---

1. Preheat oven to 400°.

2. Measure and sift all the dry ingredients together in a large bowl. Sift a second time.

3. Add 1/2 cup chopped pecans to the dry ingredients. Place the remaining pecans in a small bowl. Set aside.

4. Using the purée blade of your food processor, blend the melted soy margarine or butter, cornstarch, apple juice concentrate, Sucanat or brown sugar, salt, and egg. In a small saucepan over medium heat, heat the mixture until it thickens. The consistency should resemble thick gravy. Remove from heat, add the remaining goody ingredient (vanilla extract), and pour the mixture over the 1 cup chopped pecans. Stir to combine the ingredients. Set aside to cool.

5. Whisk the wet ingredients in a small bowl or blend them in your food processor using the purée blade.

6. Pour the wet ingredients into the dry ingredients. Stir just until mixed. *Do not overstir.*

7. Spoon the batter into greased or papered baking tins, filling each tin only about 2/3 full. Leave room for the goodie mixture.

8. Generously spoon the goodie mixture over each muffin. You should use all the mixture on 12 muffins.

9. Bake for 15–20 minutes.

**Serving suggestions:** Many Southerners enjoy their pecan pie hot, with a scoop of vanilla ice cream melting all over it. Try *Easy-Living Southern Pecan Muffins* the same way. You may want to slice the muffins and fan the slices on your favorite dessert dishes. Chase this treat with a nice hot cup of tea. Mmm. Mmm. Christmas in the South.

# Fruitcake Muffins

*Last year, I decided to make a fruitcake for everyone I know. I painted small tins in holiday colors and bought Santa stickers to decorate the lids. But when I started to purchase the ingredients, I realized I just couldn't afford everything I needed. Fruitcakes are expensive!*

*Not wanting to give up the idea entirely, I converted my favorite fruitcake recipe to Fruitcake Muffins. They are much less expensive and—to the hopeless muffin lover that I am—more satisfying than fruitcake.*

*You can use any combination of dried fruit and nuts for this recipe. My favorite is dried pineapple, dried cherries (difficult to find but worth calling around to specialty food shops), and dates, with Brazil nuts, hazelnuts, and walnuts. Prunes, raisins, dried apricots, dried apples, and tropical fruits like papaya work well, too. Slivered almonds and sunflower seeds are okay, but their flavor doesn't seem to come through as well as Brazil nuts, hazelnuts, and walnuts.*

*P. S. You can find a wide assortment of dried fruit at health-food stores and food co-ops. An ever increasing variety of dried fruits is being sold at regular grocery stores. You may want to check there first. I've noticed that one major company packages what it calls "fruit bits." These are assorted dried fruits that have been diced and packaged together. Using such products makes Fruitcake Muffins quite economical and easy to make. The fruit has been chopped and diced for you.*

**Yield:** *14 muffins*

## Dry Ingredients

| | |
|---|---|
| 1 cup whole-wheat flour | 1/2 teaspoon sea salt |
| 1 cup unbleached white flour | 1 1/2 teaspoons ground cinnamon |
| 2 teaspoons baking powder | 3/4 teaspoon powdered ginger |
| 1/2 teaspoon baking soda | 1/2 teaspoon ground cloves |

## Wet Ingredients

| | |
|---|---|
| 1 cup mashed ripe bananas (about 2 whole) | 1/4 cup molasses, warmed |
| | 2 teaspoons vanilla extract |
| 1/4 cup canola oil | 2 teaspoons brandy extract |
| 2 eggs | 2 tablespoons grated orange rind |
| 1/4 cup honey, warmed | |

## Goodies

| | |
|---|---|
| 2 cups coarsely chopped mixed dried fruit | 2 cups coarsely chopped nuts/seeds |

1. Preheat oven to 400°.

2. Measure and sift the dry ingredients together in a large bowl. Sift a second time. Set aside.

3. Whisk the wet ingredients in a medium bowl or blend them in your food processor using the purée blade and place them into a medium bowl.

4. Add the goodies to the wet ingredients and stir to combine.

5. Pour the wet ingredients into the dry ingredients. Stir just until mixed. *Do not overstir.*

6. Spoon the batter into greased or papered baking tins. Fill each cup nearly to the top.

7. Bake for 15–20 minutes.

8. Cool in the baking tins for at least 10 minutes. Remove from the tins and brush the top of each muffin with canola oil.

**Serving suggestions:** Try *Fruitcake Muffins* with your favorite holiday cider.

# Marsi's Cappuccino Muffins

*"So what kind of muffin would you like?" I asked my sister Marlene. (I call her Marsi.) "I've got Fruitcake, Cappuccino . . . "*

*"You can stop right there; I'll have a Cappuccino Muffin."*

*"Well, now, wait. There's more. I've got Rum Raisin, and Waldorf, and . . . "*

*" That's okay. I'll have a Cappuccino Muffin."*

*" . . . and Orange Cranberry, and Sunny Banana Bran, and . . . "*

*"GLORIA! You are not listening to me. I'll have a Cappuccino Muffin."*

*"Okay, Okay," I said. " I'm sorry. I didn't realize it meant that much to you."*

*If you are a cappuccino lover like Marlene (aka Marsi), these are the muffins for you!*

**Yield:** *12 muffins*

| Dry Ingredients | Wet Ingredients |
| --- | --- |
| 3 cups whole-wheat pastry flour | 1 cup triple strength coffee, cooled |
| 1/2 cup unbleached white flour | 3/4 cup low-fat sour cream |
| 2 teaspoons baking powder | 1/4 cup canola oil |
| 1 teaspoon baking soda | 1 egg |
| 1/2 teaspoon sea salt | 1/2 cup honey, warmed |
| 3 tablespoons cocoa powder | 1 teaspoon vanilla extract |
| 1/2 cup Sucanat or brown sugar | |
| 1 teaspoon ground cinnamon | |

1. Preheat oven to 400°.

2. Measure and sift the dry ingredients together in a large bowl. Sift a second time. Set aside.

3. Whisk the wet ingredients in a medium bowl or blend them in your food processor using the purée blade.

4. Pour the wet ingredients into the dry ingredients. Stir just until mixed. *Do not overstir.*

5. Spoon the batter into greased or papered baking tins. Fill each cup nearly to the top.

6. Bake for 15–20 minutes.

7. Cool in the baking tins for at least 10 minutes. Remove from the tins and brush the top of each muffin with canola oil.

**Serving suggestions:** Enjoy *Cappuccino Muffins* with a glass of egg nog. These muffins are a wonderful topper for any holiday meal, and they make a festive holiday breakfast.

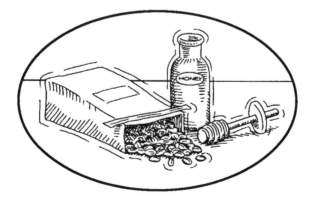

# My Mincemeat Muffins

*I have searched high and low but have yet to find a sugarless prepared mincemeat. Every product I see contains mostly refined sugar, high fructose corn syrup, etc. Frankly, I just don't understand it. The dried fruit itself is so full of natural sugar that one doesn't need to add much sweetener, refined or otherwise.*

*Years ago, I decided to come up with my own recipe for mincemeat and I am glad I did. It is so much better than any I have tasted. I love it in holiday mincemeat pies but, hey, why not a muffin?*

**Yield:** *12 muffins*

| Dry Ingredients | Wet Ingredients |
| --- | --- |
| 1 1/2 cups whole-wheat pastry flour | 1/2 cup orange juice concentrate |
| 1/2 cup unbleached white flour | 1/4 cup canola oil |
| 1/2 cup brown-rice flour | 1 egg |
| 2 teaspoons baking powder | 1/2 teaspoon vanilla extract |
| 1 teaspoon baking soda | 1 teaspoon rum extract |
| 1/2 teaspoon sea salt | |

| Goodies |
| --- |
| 2 cups mincemeat (see recipe for *Gloria's Glorious Mincement* on page 212.) |

1. Preheat oven to 375°.

2. Measure and sift the dry ingredients together in a large bowl. Sift a second time. Set aside.

3. Whisk the wet ingredients in a medium bowl or blend them in your food processor using the purée blade.

4. Add the goodies to the wet ingredients and stir to combine.

5. Pour the wet ingredients into the dry ingredients. Stir just until mixed. *Do not overstir.*

6. Spoon the batter into greased or papered baking tins. Fill each cup nearly to the top.

7. Bake for 15–20 minutes.

8. Cool in the baking tins for at least 10 minutes. Remove from the tins and brush the top of each muffin with canola oil.

**Serving suggestions:** Cut My Mincemeat Muffins into four or five slices. Arrange them nicely on a dessert plate and garnish with sliced star fruit.

# Gloria's Glorious Mincemeat

**Yield:** *approximately 4 cups*

1/2 cup chopped walnuts
1 1/2 cups chopped mixed dried fruit
   (6-ounce bag fruit bits)
1 cup diced apples
1/2 cup naturally sweetened fruit juice (any kind)
1/4 cup Sucanat or brown sugar
2 tablespoons molasses
1 cup water
1 tablespoon fresh ginger
   (1 teaspoon if powdered ginger)
1/2 teaspoon ground cinnamon
1/4 teaspoon ground cloves
1 teaspoon orange rind
1 teaspoon lemon rind

1. Place the chopped walnuts in a small bowl. Set aside.
2. Place the chopped dried fruit in a medium saucepan.
3. Core the apples and chop them into 1-inch chunks. (You do not need to peel them.) Using the purée blade of your food procesor, chop the apples into smaller bits. (If you do not have a food processor,

chop the apples by hand.) Do not grate them.
Remove the apples from the food processor and
place them in the saucepan with the dried fruit.

4. Add all the remaining ingredients to the saucepan.
   Bring to a boil. Reduce heat. Simmer for 30 minutes.
5. Add the walnuts. Stir.
6. Cool to room temperature before using.

# Old-Fashioned Ginger Currant Muffins

*When I was a kid, my mom often packed ginger biscuits with cream cheese in my school lunch pail. Sometimes my sisters and I enjoyed them as afterschool snacks. What a treat!*

*Last year, I found myself in a quaint 18th century tea shop just outside London. My English friend Jill and I savored ginger cakes topped with currants and clotted cream. We sat at a wee table where centuries of travellers before us had enjoyed similar fare. The timelessness of it all helped to rekindle my love affair with gingery baked goods.*

*It took me some time to capture the combination of ginger, spices, and molasses that makes me feel like that happy little girl at lunch time and that contented English traveller . . . but I found it.*

**Yield:** *12 muffins*

| Dry Ingredients | Wet Ingredients |
|---|---|
| 1 1/2 cups whole-wheat flour | 1 1/4 cups apple juice concentrate |
| 1 1/2 cups unbleached white flour | 1/2 cup soy or cow's milk |
| 1/2 cup brown-rice flour | 1/2 cup canola oil |
| 2 teaspoons baking powder | 1 egg |
| 1 teaspoon baking soda | 1/2 cup molasses |
| 1/4 teaspoon sea salt | 1 tablespoon grated orange rind |
| 1 teaspoon ground cinnamon | 2 tablespoons grated ginger root |
| 1/2 teaspoon ground nutmeg | (or 1 tablespoon powdered ginger) |

## Goodies

1 1/2 cups currants

1. Preheat oven to 400°.

2. Measure and sift the dry ingredients together in a large bowl. Sift a second time. Set aside.

3. Whisk the wet ingredients in a medium bowl or blend them in your food processor using the purée blade.

4. Add the goodies to the wet ingredients and stir to combine.

5. Pour the wet ingredients into the dry ingredients. Stir just until mixed. *Do not overstir.*

6. Spoon the batter into greased or papered baking tins. Fill each cup nearly to the top.

7. Bake for 15–20 minutes.

8. Cool in the baking tins for at least 10 minutes. Remove from the tins and brush the top of each muffin with canola oil.

*Serving suggestions:* To add a nice touch, try these with lemon jelly or lemon curd.

# Pumpkin Pumpkin-Seed Muffins

*Pumpkin seeds often get separated from the pumpkin and thrown out. What a shame—because pumpkin pulp and pumpkin seeds go well together; they were born that way.*

*With my Pumpkin Pumpkin-Seed Muffins, I've put the seeds back in the pumpkin and added a few goodies to boot.*

**Yield:** *14 muffins or about 40 mini-muffins*

| Dry Ingredients | Wet Ingredients |
|---|---|
| 3/4 cup whole-wheat flour | 1 1/4 cups apple juice |
| 1 cup unbleached white flour | 1/4 cup canola oil |
| 1/2 cup brown-rice flour | 1 egg |
| 2 teaspoons baking powder | 1 tablespoon molasses, warmed |
| 1 teaspoon baking soda | |
| 2 teaspoons ground cinnamon | |
| 1 teaspoon ground nutmeg | |
| 1/2 teaspoon sea salt | |
| 1/2 cup Sucanat or brown sugar | |

## Goodies

1 1/4 cups mashed pumpkin
   (about 1 pound)
1 cup roasted pumpkin seeds
3/4 cup raisins

1. Preheat oven to 400°.

2. Measure and sift the dry ingredients together in a large bowl. Sift a second time. Set aside.

3. Whisk the wet ingredients in a medium bowl or blend them in your food processor using the purée blade.

4. Add the mashed pumpkin to the wet ingredients and blend or whisk to a smooth consistency. Add the remaining goody ingredients (seeds and raisins) to the wet ingredients and stir to combine.

5. Pour the wet ingredients into the dry ingredients. Stir just until mixed. *Do not overstir.*

6. Spoon the batter into greased or papered baking tins. Fill each cup nearly to the top.

7. Bake for 15–20 minutes for regular muffins or 10–15 minutes for mini-muffins.

8. Cool in the baking tins for at least 10 minutes. Remove from the tins and brush the top of each muffin with canola oil.


*Serving suggestions:* Place a basket full of mini *Pumpkin Pumpkin-Seed Muffins* on your holiday table between the steamed broccoli and the cranberry sauce. Your table will look like a bouquet of fall flowers.

# Rum Raisin Muffins

*Eggnog. Yum, Yum! Don't you just love it! Eggnog with a shot of fire water (demon rum, that is) and a dash of nutmeg makes the holidays authentic. Now you can enjoy the flavor of eggnog with rum and nutmeg in this holiday muffin. I've used rum extract rather than the real thing because alcohol puts a damper on muffins. It reacts in funny ways with the rising agents and makes muffins go flat.*

**Yield:** *12 muffins*

| Dry Ingredients | Wet Ingredients |
|---|---|
| 1 1/4 cups whole-wheat flour | 3/4 cup apple juice concentrate |
| 1 3/4 cups unbleached white flour | 1 1/4 cups soy or cow's milk |
| 2 teaspoons baking powder | 1/2 cup soy margarine or |
| 1 teaspoon baking soda | butter, melted |
| 1/2 teaspoon sea salt | 1 egg |
| 1 teaspoon ground nutmeg | 1 teaspoon vanilla extract |
| 1/4 teaspoon ground cardamom | 2 1/2 teaspoons rum extract |
| | 1 teaspoon grated lemon rind |

| Goodies |
|---|
| 1 1/2 cups raisins |

1. Preheat oven to 400°.

2. Measure and sift the dry ingredients together in a large bowl. Sift a second time. Set aside.

3. Whisk the wet ingredients in a medium bowl or blend them in your food processor using the purée blade.

4. Add the raisins to the wet ingredients and stir to combine.

5. Pour the wet ingredients into the dry ingredients. Stir just until mixed. *Do not overstir.*

6. Spoon the batter into greased or papered baking tins. Fill each cup nearly to the top.

7. Bake for 15–20 minutes.

8. Cool in the baking tins for at least 10 minutes. Remove from the tins and brush the top of each muffin with canola oil.

**Serving suggestions:** Try *Rum Raisin Muffins* for dessert with *Vanilla Custard Sauce* (see *Gloria's Glorious Muffin Sauces* on page 152) and whipped cream. Or enjoy *Rum Raisin Muffins* with the main course of your holiday meals.

# Stuffin' Muffins

*I'm a bread-stuffing-lover from way back. I don't wait for a holiday; I make bread stuffing anytime—just to eat with vegetables and gravy or with a salad and stewed fruit. Thus, you see, Stuffin' Muffins were a must for this cookbook. Bread stuffing in a muffin. Who could ask for more?*

*I even use bread crumbs in the recipe. When you make these muffins, take care to use only coarse bread crumbs prepared from leftover bread. If you do not have leftover bread, do not use heavy store-bought bread crumbs. They will make the muffins too heavy and dense. Rather, substitute 3/4 cup additional flour for the bread crumbs in this recipe.*

**Yield:** *12 muffins*

| Dry Ingredients | Wet Ingredients |
| --- | --- |
| 3/4 cup whole-wheat flour | 1 cup vegetable broth |
| 1 cup unbleached white flour | 1/2 cup soy or cow's milk |
| 1 cup coarse bread crumbs | 1/2 cup olive oil |
| (from leftover bread) | 1 egg |
| 2 teaspoons baking powder | 1 tablespoon honey, warmed |
| 1 teaspoon baking soda | |
| 1/2 teaspoon sea salt | |

### Goodies

| | |
| --- | --- |
| 1/4 cup coarsely chopped walnuts | 2 cloves minced garlic |
| 1/2 cup chopped celery | 1/4 cup roasted sunflower seeds |
| 1/2 cup chopped onion | 1/4 cup raisins |
| 2 teaspoons chopped fresh parsley | 1/2 teaspoon rubbed sage |
| (1 teaspoon if dried parsley) | 1/2 teaspoon ground thyme |
| 1/2 cup grated sharp cheddar cheese | |

1. Preheat oven to 400°.

2. Measure and sift all the dry ingredients *except the bread crumbs* together in a large bowl. Sift a second time. Add the bread crumbs and toss. Set aside.

3. Whisk the wet ingredients in a medium bowl or blend them in your food processor using the purée blade.

4. Add the goodies to the wet ingredients and stir to combine.

5. Pour the wet ingredients into the dry ingredients. Stir just until mixed. *Do not overstir.*

6. Spoon the batter into greased or papered baking tins. Fill each cup nearly to the top.

7. Bake for 15–20 minutes.

8. Cool in the baking tins for at least 10 minutes. Remove from the tins and brush the top of each muffin with olive oil.

**Serving suggestions:** Serve these as you would stuffin' stuffin'.

# Sweet Potato Carob Chip Muffins

*Not long ago, someone served me pumpkin pie with chocolate chips on top. It was good, but I found the pumpkin too limp a match for the overpowering chocolate. The combination inspired me to improve on it.*

*Being a North Carolinian, I naturally thought of sweet potatoes. (North Carolina is the sweet potato capital of the United States.) I find the flavor of sweet potato to be sweeter, deeper, and richer than that of pumpkin. And carob offers a flavor that is similar to chocolate but not nearly as overwhelming.*

*Thus were born Sweet Potato Carob Chip Muffins. Sounds like a crazy combination, but, oh, wow!*

**Yield:** *16 muffins*

| Dry Ingredients | Wet Ingredients |
|---|---|
| 1 cup whole-wheat flour | 1/2 cup apple juice concentrate |
| 1 1/2 cups unbleached white flour | 1/2 cup soy or cow's milk |
| 1 tablespoon baking powder | 1 1/4 cups mashed sweet potato |
| 1/2 teaspoon baking soda | (about 1 pound) |
| 1/2 teaspoon sea salt | 1/4 cup canola oil |
| 1 1/2 teaspoons ground cinnamon | 1 egg |
| 1/4 teaspoon ground cloves | 1/2 cup honey, warmed |
| 1/2 teaspoon ground allspice | |
| 1/2 teaspoon ground nutmeg | |

| Goodies | |
|---|---|
| 1 1/4 cups coarsely chopped pecans | 1 1/4 cups carob chips |

1. Preheat oven to 400°.

2. Measure and sift the dry ingredients together in a large bowl. Sift a second time. Set aside.

3. Add the goodies to the dry ingredients and toss.

4. Whisk the wet ingredients in a small bowl or blend them in your food processor using the purée blade.

5. Pour the wet ingredients into the dry ingredients. Stir just until mixed. *Do not overstir.*

6. Spoon the batter into greased or papered baking tins. Fill each cup nearly to the top.

7. Bake for 15–20 minutes.

8. Cool in the baking tins for at least 10 minutes. Remove from the tins and brush the top of each muffin with canola oil.


***Serving suggestions:*** Once I accidently-on-purpose dropped a scoop of frozen vanilla yogurt on these. The combination was outrageous!

# Waldorf Muffins

*Waldorf salad is one of my favorite fruity accompaniments for holiday meals. Somehow the combination of apples, raisins, celery, and nuts captures everything that I think about when I think about fall holiday menus.*

*I use dried and fresh apples as well as apple juice concentrate to give depth to the apple-ness of Waldorf Muffins.*

**Yield:** *12 muffins*

| Dry Ingredients | Wet Ingredients |
| --- | --- |
| 1 1/4 cups whole-wheat flour | 1/2 cup apple juice concentrate |
| 1 cup unbleached white flour | 1 cup soy or cow's milk |
| 1/4 cup amaranth flour | 1/4 cup canola oil |
| 2 teaspoons baking powder | 1 egg |
| 1 teaspoon baking soda | 1 teaspoon grated lemon rind |
| 1/2 teaspoon sea salt | |

### Goodies

1/4 cup chopped dried apples

1 cup chopped celery

1/2 cup chopped fresh apples (about 1 small whole) *Do not grate.*

1/2 cup coarsely chopped roasted walnuts

3/4 cup raisins

1. Preheat oven to 400°.

2. Measure and sift the dry ingredients together in a large bowl. Sift a second time. Set aside.

3. Whisk the wet ingredients in a medium bowl or blend them in your food processor using the purée blade and place them in a medium bowl.

4. Add the goodies to the wet ingredients and stir to combine.

5. Pour the wet ingredients into the dry ingredients. Stir just until mixed. *Do not overstir.*

6. Spoon the batter into greased or papered baking tins. Fill each cup nearly to the top.

7. Bake for 15–20 minutes.

8. Cool in the baking tins for at least 10 minutes. Remove from the tins and brush the top of each muffin with canola oil.

*Serving suggestions: Waldorf Muffins* are great throughout the year. Carry them along with summer picnics, to the pool, or the beach. They are great at backyard picnics on Memorial Day and the Fourth of July.

# EPILOGUE

*Having well polished the whole bow, he added a golden tip.*

Homer
*Illiad, Book IV*

A t the end of a work of fiction, there's sometimes an epilogue that tells readers what happened to the characters after the book ended. After *this* book ends, its characters—the glorious muffins—will be vanishing from your plates. There will be that rare—extremely rare—occasion when you have leftover muffins. Of course, you can crumble them and toss them out the back door for the birds to enjoy. That's always a nice offering. Or you can recycle them for human consumption.

I recycle both sweet and savory leftover muffins to make muffin pudding. *Sweet Muffin Pudding* for breakfast is a fun change from hot cereal, eggs, or regular muffins. And it makes a delicious dessert. Depending on the type of leftover sweet muffins, I add apples, dried fruit, and nuts to enhance that sweet muffin goodness.

*Savory Muffin Pudding* is a meal in itself—kind of like a quiche with stuffing. Again, depending on the type of leftover savory muffin, I add vegetables—like broccoli, onions, corn, carrots, and peas—plus nuts and cheese.

# Sweet Muffin Pudding

| Dry ingredients | Wet ingredients |
|---|---|
| 2 cups leftover sweet muffins | 1/2 cup apple juice concentrate |
| up to 1/2 cup chopped apples | 1 cup soy or cow's milk |
| up to 1/2 cup chopped dried fruit | 2 eggs |
| up to 1/2 cup chopped nuts | 2 tablespoons honey or |
| 1/4 teaspoon salt | molasses, warmed |
| 1/2 teaspoon ground cinnamon | 2 teaspoons vanilla extract |
| 1/2 teaspoon ground nutmeg | 1/2 teaspoon rum or brandy extract |
| | 2 teaspoons grated lemon or |
| | orange rind |
| | 1 tablespoon soy margarine |
| | or butter |

1. Preheat oven to 350°.

2. Generously grease a 1-quart casserole.

3. Crumble the leftover muffins in the bottom of the pan.

4. Sprinkle the apples, dried fruit, nuts, salt, and spices over the muffins. Toss the mixture to combine all the ingredients.

5. Whisk all the wet ingredients *except the margarine or butter* in a medium bowl or blend them in your food processor using the purée blade. Pour the mixture over the crumbled muffin mixture. Dot with margarine or butter.

6. Bake for about 45 minutes.

**Serving Suggestions:** For breakfast, serve *Sweet Muffin Pudding* with a drizzle of maple syrup or honey. You may also want to try it with your favorite yogurt—fruity or plain. For dessert, serve *Sweet Muffin Pudding* plain or with a daub of vanilla yogurt, whipped cream, or ice cream.

# Savory Muffin Pudding

| Dry ingredients | Wet ingredients |
| --- | --- |
| 2 cups leftover savory muffins | 1 1/2 cups soy or cow's milk |
| up to 1/2 cup vegetables | 2 eggs |
| (chopped or grated if need be) | 1 clove minced garlic |
| up to 1/2 cup chopped nuts | 1 tablespoon soy margarine |
| up to 1 cup grated cheese | or butter |
| 1/4 teaspoon salt | |
| 1/8 teaspoon ground black pepper | |
| a sprinkling of complimentary herbs | |
| (herbs to match those in the muffins) | |

1. Preheat oven to 350°.

2. Generously grease a 1-quart casserole.

3. Crumble the leftover muffins in the bottom of the pan.

4. Sprinkle the chopped vegetables, chopped nuts, grated cheese, salt, pepper, and herbs over the muffins. Toss the mixture to combine all the ingredients.

5. Whisk all the wet ingredients *except the margarine or butter* in a medium bowl or blend them in your food processor using the purée blade. Pour the mixture over the crumbled muffin mixture. Dot with margarine or butter.

6. Bake for about 45 minutes.

**Serving Suggestions:** Serve as a side dish or enjoy *Savory Bread Pudding* with a salad. It's a meal in itself!

Of course, the muffins aren't the only "characters" in this book. There's also me, the Gloria in *Gloria's Glorious Muffins*. For me, writing this book has been a *most* enriching experience. For one thing, I've perfected the art of muffin-making (if I do say so myself), and have given my friends and relatives countless pleasure-filled moments as they have enjoyed my wholesome and nutritious treats. As I said in the beginning of this book, delighting people with muffins has become a bit of a religion with me. Baking the hundreds of muffins required to put this book together has given me plenty of opportunities to practice my religion. Now that I have shared my recipes with you, I look forward to your delighting your loved ones.

Second, I've had the pleasure of recalling special times spent with friends and relatives and remembering the delicious foods we shared. Mmm. Mmm. My mouth waters just thinking about the foods! (Taste has always been my favorite sense.) And my heart tickles thinking about the good times. I hope that you and I will create many new happy memories—while eating Gloria's Glorious Muffins, of course.

I feel as though I've cultivated a kinship with you, my readers. It's as though we've been chatting while rocking on the back porch swing or puttering around the kitchen on a cool autumn day.

And if these benefits aren't enough, I've been inspired to share my baked treasures with more people than ever. In the final months of writing *Gloria's Glorious Muffins*, I endeavored to sell my muffins at the local farmers' market. This put me in weekly contact with some of the down-home folks of my community—like Ray and his mom, farmers from "out yonder toward Asheville"; George, the beekeeper, ("You gotta taste my sourwood honey, honey. It's the best this side of the Blue Ridge."); the herb-grower from aisle three ("I tell everyone about your muffins."); and Jean and her sister in the flower booth next to mine. They all buy my muffins, and I buy their herbs, honey, nuts, fruits, and vegetables to put in my muffins. The townspeople come as early as 6:00 A.M.. to take part. I love it! I sit at my little muffin booth just a-grinnin' from ear to ear.

What can I say? The whole process has been truly glorious. May you have as much fun baking and eating muffins as I have had.

# INDEX

# INDEX

Rye flakes, 12
   used in muffins, 118
Rye flour, 11–12
   used in muffins, 90, 118, 124, 156
Rye muffins, 118

Safflower oil, 22, 23
Salt, 14
Saturated fat, 1, 22, 24
Sauces. See Gloria's Glorious Muffin Sauces.
Savory/dinner muffins, 93–147
Savory Muffin Pudding, 227, 229
Sea salt, 14
Sea-Veggie Surprise Muffins, 132
Seedy Muffins, 134
Sesame oil, 23
   used in muffins, 132, 142
Sesame seeds used in muffins, 134
Seven-Factors-of-Enlightenment Muffins, 188
Shortening, 21–22
Sifter, 5
Sifting, importance of, 5, 8
Sodium aluminum sulfate, 13–14
Soybean oil, 22, 23
Soy flour, 12
   used in muffins, 52, 70, 108, 112, 114, 124, 132, 134, 198
Soy milk, 19, 20, 21
Soy products. See Dairy and soy products.
Soysage, 80
   used in muffins, 80, 128, 136
Soysage Cheese Muffins, 80
Soysage Pizza Muffins, 136
Spanokopita Muffins, 138

Spinach used in muffins, 130, 138, 140, 144
Spinach-Lentil Muffins, 140
Spreads. See Gloria's Glorious Muffin Butters and Spreads.
Spring Roll Muffins, 142
Squash used in muffins, 164
Start-a-Movement Muffins, 82
Steven's Sun-Dried-Tomato Muffins, 144
Strawberry Muffins, 190
Stuffin' Muffins, 220
Substitutions. See Ingredient substitutions.
Sucanat, 18
   glaze, 156, 169
Sugar, refined or table
   and natural sweeteners, 15
   consumption of, 15
   equivalencies to other sweeteners, 19
   refining process, 17–18
Sulfur dioxide gas, 102
Sun-dried tomatoes, 144
   used in muffins, 136, 144
Sunflower oil, 22, 23
Sunflower seeds used in muffins, 46, 54, 76, 84, 126, 134, 156
Sunny Banana Bran Muffins, 84
Sweeteners, 14–18
   equivalencies to table sugar, 19
   See also All-fruit jam, jelly, and marmalade; Barley malt syrup; Fruit; Fruit juice; Fruit juice concentrate; Honey; Maple syrup; Molasses; Rice syrup.
Sweet Muffin Pudding, 227, 228
Sweet peas used in muffins, 128
Sweet Potato Carob Chip Muffins, 222
Sweety-Fruity Spread, 56, 89